State of Exception

State of Exception
Cultural Responses to the Rhetoric of Fear

Edited by

Elena Bellina and Paola Bonifazio

CAMBRIDGE SCHOLARS PRESS

State of Exception: Cultural Responses to the Rhetoric of Fear, edited by Elena Bellina and Paola Bonifazio

This book first published 2006 by

Cambridge Scholars Press

15 Angerton Gardens, Newcastle, NE5 2JA, UK

British Library Cataloguing in Publication Data
A catalogue record for this book is available from the British Library

ISBN 1-84718-021-3

TABLE OF CONTENTS

PREFACE

The following papers were inspired by the conference *State of Exception: Cultural Responses to the Rhetoric of Fear*, hosted by New York University's Department of Italian Studies on April 21-23 2005. The conference was sponsored by New York University's Graduate School of Arts and Science, the Dean's Office of the Graduate School of Arts and Sciences, and Casa Italiana Zerilli-Marimò. We would like to thank prof. Ruth Ben-Ghiat, Chair of the New York University Department of Italian, and prof. Virginia Cox, Director of the Graduate Students, for their generous help in organizing the conference.

We are deeply greatful to prof. Karen Pinkus for her guidance and support. Her insights were an important source of inspiration on the final structure of the book.

We also wish to thank Max Henninger, Valerie McGuire and Lindsay Eufusia, for their assistance in preparing the manuscript.

Unless otherwise noted, all translations from Italian are by the chapters' authors.

ELENA BELLINA
INTRODUCTION

The US administration's response to the terrorist attacks of September 11, 2001—a response that aims at making a generalized state of fear and confusion the basis for far-reaching legal transformations—rendered the debate at NYU particularly lively. Our discussion of what the "state of exception" implies both on the macro and on the micropolitical level was strongly informed by an awareness of Italy's long history of exceptional uses of power.

Italian philosopher Giorgio Agamben has widely elaborated on the historical effects of the juridical concept of the state of exception, recalling the definition of this concept formulated during the early 1920s by German legal theorist Carl Schmitt. According to Schmitt, the state of exception implies a "suspension of the entire existing juridical order."[1] Agamben underscores the uncertain and paradoxical character of the resulting condition. The state of exception presents itself as an inherently elusive phenomenon, a juridical no-man's land where the law is suspended in order to be preserved. The state of exception "is neither external nor internal to the juridical order, and the problem of defining it concerns a threshold, or a zone of indifference, where inside and outside do not exclude each other but rather blur with each other."[2] In this sense, the state of exception is both a structured or rule-governed and an anomic phenomenon: "The state of exception separates the norm from its application in order to make its application possible. It introduces a zone of anomie into the law in order to make the effective regulation of the real possible."[3]

Agamben argues that the state of exception was already codified in Roman law. The Roman *iustitium*—literally, "suspension of the law"—can indeed be seen as an archetypal state of exception. Whenever it judged the Roman republic to be seriously endangered, the senate could pass a decree allowing for the imposition of extraordinary legal measures. The *iustitium* was characterized by the same paradoxical void that is the defining feature of the state of exception conceptualized by Schmitt. The indeterminacy of this void raises questions about the nature of the crimes perpetrated during the *iustitium:* the suspension of the law turns these crimes into mere facts, whose definition lies outside the sphere of justice. It is also suggestive that the *iustitium* was typically declared following the death of the sovereign; the *iustitium* was a period of juridical instability resulting from the loss of the person thought to embody the law. In general, every period of mourning can be said to be characterized by a suspension of ordinary human interaction.

On the basis of his analysis of the *iustitium,* Agamben identifies four central features of the state of exception. Firstly, the state of exception is "a space devoid of law, a zone of anomie in which all legal determinations are deactivated."[4] Secondly, "this space devoid of law seems [...] to be so essential to the juridical order that it must seek in every way to assure itself a relationship with it."[5] Thirdly, the actions committed at this time cannot be legally judged because they are situated in "an absolute non-place with respect to the law."[6] Finally, the undefinability of the absence of law generates a "force or a mystical element…that both…the constituted power [and] the constituent power seek to appropriate."[7]

The juridical tensions inherent in the state of exception necessitate a constant interplay of anomie and nomos, an ongoing interaction between order and the suspension of order that can be used to justify every conceivable abuse of power. Such interplay, epitomized by the aftermath of the 2001 terrorist attacks in the USA, has become a central—and perhaps even the defining—element in today's geopolitical scenario. As Agamben points out:

> The state of exception has today reached its maximum worldwide deployment. The normative aspect of law can thus be obliterated and contradicted with impunity by a governmental violence that—while ignoring international law externally and producing a permanent state of exception internally—nevertheless still claims to be applying the law.[8]

In a globalized world exposed to ever more dramatic dangers, the established legal order goes into crisis and the rhetoric of fear is deployed to legitimate a seemingly endless series of states of exception. The papers collected in this volume explore the ways in which human and civil rights are suspended as fear is used to justify exceptional legal procedures. Throughout the centuries, Italy has experienced many such historical moments of crisis—moments in which political, economic, and cultural authorities have made fear a central component of their strategies for producing consensus. Italy also has a rich tradition of intellectuals subverting such strategies by turning the rhetoric of fear back upon itself and against power. The papers collected here explore some of the most important aspects of such cultural responses to the rhetoric of fear. Most papers focus on the second half of the twentieth century, a period that was particularly troublesome for Italy.

This book is divided into three parts. The first part explores philosophical issues related to the history of the state of exception within the frame of juridical, political, and economical principles. The second part focuses on cultural and literary production during times of socio-political crisis, devoting special attention to the ways in which history may interact with its fictional representations. The third section is devoted to the literary and cinematic representations of the biopolitical effects of the state of exception on urban areas and the spectacularization of terrorism in Italian cinema.

Karen Pinkus opens the first part with a careful investigation of how the state of exception functions not just on the levels of juridical and executive power, but also on those of the aesthetic and the symbolic. In "$, Anomie, State of Exception," Pinkus reflects on the stock market crash of 8 July 2002—the most dramatic since September 11—in order to analyze the ways in which anomie manifests itself on the marketplace, in relation to money, and in production. Pinkus examines how issues related to anomie have been analyzed and represented at different moments in the history of Italian cultural production, from Cesare Beccaria's economic treatises to the films of Antonioni.

Paolo Matteucci explores the relationship between the juridical concept of the state of exception and the production of space. In "Sovereignty, Borders, Exception," Matteucci reflects on the new nature of borders in the aftermath of September 11, relating these claims to the transformations the concept of the border has undergone since antiquity. The Roman concept of *terminus* becomes a theoretical tool for analyzing the spatial actualization of the state of exception.

Andrea Benino brings Antonio Negri into the debate on the state of exception, drawing a comparison between Negri's *operaista* analyses and Agamben's reflections on biopolitics. In "From Stato-Piano to Stato-Crisi: Proletarian Self-Valorization and the State of Exception," Benino discusses three militant works written by Negri in the 1970s—*Partito operaio contro il lavoro* (1973), *Proletari e stato* (1975), *Il dominio e il sabotaggio* (1977)— in order to explore the relationship between Negri's concept of *stato-crisi* and Agamben's reflections on the state of exception.

In "*La morte come pena:* Law, Death Penalty and State of Exception," Maurizio Vito accounts for the introduction of the death penalty in the Italian penal system of the Middle Ages. Evoking a tradition of critical thought that ranges from Benjamin to Derrida, Vito's reading of *La morte come pena. Saggio sulla violenza legale* by Italo Mereu demonstrates how a practice such as that of the death penalty becomes possible only when the law opens up to the anomic space of the exception.

Max Henninger opens the second part by offering a thorough description of the prolonged state of exception undergone by the Italian republic during the 1970s. "Patchwork, 1979: Notes on *Blackout* by Nanni Balestrini" analyzes a poem written by Nanni Balestrini immediately before his escape to France; Balestrini had been charged with complicity in the activites of the terrorist Red Brigades. Henninger explores the peculiarities of *Blackout* by confronting the poem with its historical context and a variety of theoretical models ranging from the Italian Marxism of the 1960s and 1970s to the theory of space elaborated by Gilles Deleuze and Félix Guattari.

In "Useppe's State of Exception in Elsa Morante's *History*," Marisa Giorgi presents Morante's novel as an emblematic case of how the state of exception may be represented in fiction. Set during the historical state of exception that was World War II, Morante's narrative also portrays exceptional social, physical, and mental conditions such as that of the character Useppe, a child whose inability to speak epitomizes the seclusion and irrationality generated by the suspension of order.

Chiara Sartori reflects on the construction of national identity, exploring the peculiar case of *triestinità*. In "Trieste Borderline Identity," she analyzes important moments in the economic and literary history of Trieste, applying theories elaborated by Claudio Magris and Paolo Rumiz to the processes of cultural assimilation and interaction.

In the first contribution to the third section of this volume, Paola Bonifazio confronts the anomic space of the concentration camp with the suburbs of post-war Italian industrial cities, exploring the cinematic representations of those biopolitical areas where naked life becomes an object of power. Bonifazio analyzes state-sponsored documentary films on 1950s urban reconstruction, as well as Luchino Visconti's *Rocco and his brothers* (1960) and PierPaolo Pasolini's *Accattone* (1961), exposing the role played by state propaganda during a period of profound socio-economic transformation.

Alan O'Leary's "Ordinary People (*Lest We Forget*)" focuses on the spectacularization of late-1970s terrorist violence. Recalling Guy Debord's observations on the "society of the spectacle" and Agamben's remarks on the inherently spectacular nature of terrorist action, O'Leary questions the representation of the 1980 bombing of Bologna's central train station provided in *Lest We Forget* (*Per non dimenticare*). This short film, sponsored by Italian national television, presents the paradox of a commemorative visual project setting out to condemn a terrorist massacre by means of an inherently spectacular medium—a medium that always risks becoming complicit with terrorism's own spectacularization of violence.

Investigating the mechanisms by which the suspension of order functions historically, politically, and culturally, these papers open up new spaces for debate on the role played by the state of exception in Italian culture.

PART I

STATE OF EXCEPTION: THEORY AND PRACTICE

CHAPTER ONE

KAREN PINKUS

$, ANOMIE, STATE OF EXCEPTION

Monetary Aporias

During the week of July 8, 2002 the U.S. stock market experienced its worst decline since the week following the terrorist acts of September 11. Analysts attributed this decline to a loss of confidence in corporate America following a series of high profile revelations of malfeasance in accounting. President George W. Bush gave a speech (orchestrated by Karl Rove) on Tuesday, July 9th, vowing to overhaul the practices of reporting, and proposed legislation that would force chief financial or executive officers of corporations to sign off on their quarterly and annual reports of income, suggesting a greater fiduciary relationship with the public. However, public reaction to the speech was lukewarm, and some critics argued that Bush and members of his administration (indeed, most of the political elites in the U.S.) are so thoroughly enmeshed in insider information that the President could not possibly speak clearly on the topic. In the wake of the plunge, analysts talked about the "disappearance of vast wealth." Where did this wealth go? On one level, this is clearly a question for economists and not for humanists. They would have an answer—but it might not be the one to satisfy our pessimism. Rhetorically, at least, the market crash seems to satisfy a certain definition of dematerialization. Wealth that was previously *there,* present, in existence on the scene of the market disappeared. But what was this wealth and where did it go? It was nothing material, since as long as it was invested in equities listed on the stock exchanges, it was neither money nor commodities. So, once again, what is wealth? It is a potential for something not yet realized that was diminished, or indeed, entirely dissipated, after the week of red arrows. What was experienced was a dematerialization of something non-material inasmuch as not-yet-material. Wealth moved to a non-space and a non-time in which "inside and outside indetermine one another," during a state of emergency, declared not by a single sovereign national figure, but by the sovereign conventionality of the community of international investors; not in response to any declaration of a (new) war, poor unemployment numbers, dipping consumer confidence, or disappointing earnings. Rather, as Christian Marazzi might say, investors performed an act that underscored their communal body as predominantly linguistic.

I type in my credit card number for an online purchase. In the temporal interregnum when my account is debited and the amount of the purchase credited to a service provider, *my* money, earned by *my* labor, academic as it may be, exists in that state known in economic terms as the float, an indeterminate non-time and non-space, apparently ephemeral, yet in global monetary terms, highly profitable and volatile.

The float, the dematerialization of wealth: what are the spatial or temporal boundaries that mark these conditions? In the infinite struggle to extend the nanometrics of the float, how do we know when it is over? Where is the threshold within which wealth can be said to have "reappeared"? I am interested in thinking about the monetary realm in general. The dollar sign in my title is there to signify money, but specifically the synecdochic relation of all money to the U.S. dollar. The interstitial space and time when money undergoes a syncope is quite mysterious, especially in the digital age. Can the concepts that Giorgio Agamben develops in *Homo Sacer* and *Stato di eccezione* help to demystify this realm?

Although complex and heterogeneous, at its core Agamben's work on the "state of exception" lies in a conversation between Carl Schmitt and Walter Benjamin around the question of a pure, potentially revolutionary or divine violence (*reine Gewalt*) existing outside of any juridical context.[1] Schmitt argues that there is no pure violence, because it is included in law by its very exclusion, by the sovereign decision, which Benjamin does not admit. Rather, for Benjamin, the state of exception is a zone of interdetermination and catastrophe, not part of the juridical order, yet increasingly common in the modern world. Writing in 1942, Benjamin notes that the "state of exception" has become the norm. Agamben continues that in the new millennium, it has become permanent. It is useless to try to delimit the state of exception by strengthening the spatial and temporal boundaries of law, since there is no law "out there" that exists independently of its dialectical relationship with the state of exception. In other words, any politics (neo) liberal or otherwise, that pretends to get rid of the state of exception or appropriate it for those against whom violence has been perpetuated is deluded. All we can do is to patiently unmask its fictiveness, and to "attempt to interrupt the machine that is leading us to a global civil war," Agamben concludes.[2] We will not return to a pure originary state, but rather a "new condition" of possibility.[3]

Extending the State of Exception?

Before proceeding on this course, I must admit that for me the very question of the extension of the seductive concept "the state of exception" beyond the realm of the concentration camp, of juridical politics and executive powers into spheres such as the aesthetic or the symbolic, is quite vexed. I use the term "seductive" because in one sense, this term would seem to open up significant temporal and spatial potentialities. It has been invoked, for instance, in the context of actual debates on the status of "exceptional" detainees in that exceptional place that is Guantánamo.[4] Zygmunt Bauman has likewise utilized the "state of exception" to discuss refugees in Europe, especially those housed in what are called in Italian *centri temporanei di permanenza* (found in exceptional places like Lampedusa).[5] But we should be cautious. The "state of exception" risks being applied indiscriminately to any irregularity, any moment of panic, any grey zone, such that it may be used by the "enemy" as well as by "us." In other words, this term could shed its complex historical and philological genealogy and become, merely, a synonym for any ambiguity or ambivalence.[6]

Similarly, "state of exception" could be a crucial concept for scholarly work around the "national languages." We might use the term in a positive sense, to refer to research in areas such as border or postcolonial studies, diaspora or immigrant cultures; or in order to problematize the traditional and restrictive disciplinary divisions to which we might be forced to adhere in our institutional affiliations. At the same time, "state of exception" might fall into the hands of those "others"—such as university administrators—bent on extracting surplus value from scholars by supporting what they call interdisciplinarity at the expense of work, no matter how relevant, in a particular national idiom. In the American context, university administrators fixate on centers (overlapping areas of research) and sites of synergy. The potential violence that pertains to the Agambenian "state of exception" is no where to be found. Rather, the "center" is at best a purely interstitial zone. Our job, then, is to keep in mind the catastrophic and violent qualities of the state of exception that might be suppressed in everyday use of the term.

As so often in the work we do, we find ourselves facing a question of translation. That is, a literal translation of Agamben's phrase, "state of exception," places the emphasis on exceptionality, from the Latin *ex+capere,* to take hold of. Exceptionality supposes a seizing, rather than a passive acceptance of a state of being. As Agamben notes, it is not merely a drawing of boundaries but a forceful and willful taking out, that creates the exception.

If, rather than translating literally, we take up the equivalent English terms emergency powers, state of emergency (most notably seen on our television screens in the wake of Hurricane Katrina) or martial law, our sphere of operation seem to be more policy-oriented and less philosophical; more concretely contained and less abstractly potential. For instance, in the United States, the declaration of a state of emergency on the part of local governments functions at a practical level to open the way for state and federal declarations, for fast-track funding, to allow authorization of extraordinary allocation to first responders, or to defer property taxes for the effected individuals, even in cases where there is no loss of life or apparent "tragedy." The state of emergency has entered our everyday vocabulary as a synonym for "bureaucratic expediency." The current "state of emergency," then, far from being a suspension of law ("how can an anomie be inscribed within the juridical order?" Agamben asks with regard to the idea that the simple topography of "inside" and "outside" is insufficient to explain the phenomenon)[7] would seem to be a heightened state of law in which governments work efficiently, cutting through red tape. The declaration of martial law, similarly, allows the military and authorized personnel to "do their jobs" as in New Orleans, when—at least according to media reports—"marauding gangs of looters" and gunshots fired in the Superdome seemed to impede progress.

So much depends, then, on whether we use the term "state of exception" as one with immediate, performative, and practical implications. The more we delve into Agamben's work, the more it becomes clear that the temporal and the spatial intersect one another in complex ways, so they cannot authentically be separated. Moreover, we see that at the heart of the concept is the question of the place of an anomic violence. Inasmuch as a dictionary definition of anomie implies laziness, stupor, or lack of action, anomic violence might seem oxymoronic, or at least contradictory. But as we will see, in context, anomie does not mean a suspension of positive action so much as a suspension of law that is, however, included in law.

Anomie and Money

One of Agamben's concrete examples in the temporal realm is the period of Roman law called *iustitium.* Acts performed during this period of juridical *tempus mortuum* can be said to be characterized by anomie. He who acts during the *iustitium,* "neither executes nor transgress the law, but *inexecutes* [*inesegue*] it. His actions, in this sense, are mere facts, the appraisal of which, once the *iustitium* is expired, will depend on the circumstances."[8] The *iustitium* is linked with a period of mourning, as for a dead king or pope, prior to the conclave to elect a new pope, for instance.

Anomie comes from the Greek *anomia,* meaning lawlessness, *a-nomos*. It is the opposite of the word nimble, in English. Nimble derives from *nemein,* to distribute or manage; to be quick, light, alert, responsive; linked to *nomos* as usage, custom, law. A-nomie, as in Durkheim, suggests a social instability resulting from a breakdown of standards and values; personal unrest, alienation, lack of purpose or ideals. In *The Division of Labour in Society,* Durkheim wrote that over time, as society becomes more complex social bonds break down. Periods of disruption (economic depression, for instance) bring about greater anomie and higher rates of crime, suicide, and deviance. In one sense, anomie is unbridled desire. Durkheim writes:

> If the rules of the conjugal morality lose their authority, and the mutual obligations of husband and wife become less respected, the emotions and appetites ruled by this sector of morality will become unrestricted and uncontained, and accentuated by this very release; powerless to fulfill themselves because they have been freed from all limitations, these emotions will produce a disillusionment which manifests itself visibly...[9]

Durkheim is careful to assert that anomie is not the normal state of affairs in modern labor. It is a pathological psychological state, or, a state of exception, used in the most generic sense. Some readers have used Durkheim to support the idea that in the development of industrial production, such pathology was an innovation. Indeed, Durkheim is often credited with inventing the term, but this is, of course, a convenient fiction which would allow us to understand the social order resulting from the Industrial Revolution as something particular that might indeed disappear with new forms of production or new markets.

In reality anomie is an older word, used in a variety of contexts prior to the "invention of modern ethnography." Mill, for instance, was preoccupied with the lack of desire of among the English in the mid-nineteenth century. Prior to Mill, the Italian Enlightenment thinker, Cesare Beccaria, best known for *Dei Delitti e delle pene,* also authored a lengthy work on political economy, *Elementi di economia pubblica* (based on his lessons of 1769 and years following but published later). The very definition of public economy, for Beccaria, lies, like all of the arts and sciences, in desire, or more precisely, the "desire of being distinguished, that of shunning what the French term *ennui* and so forth."[10] He goes on to explain: "For in the state of society, while we learn to supply our natural wants with more facility, the frequency of our intercourse gives new activity to our faculties, and augments the number of our desires."[11]

Beccaria notes that a nation which produces precious metals is fortunate indeed, and such nations have always been "either the manifest or secret conquerors of the universe."[12] But he consoles himself with the fact that the real politicians have always looked more favorably upon acquiring gold than upon possessing it as a natural resource since acquisition requires motion, action, labor, which are at the heart of any political body. "Those nations that possess gold as a natural resource can be said to possess a drug that numbs all industry or productivity."[13] In a discussion of the Spanish in his *Treatise,* he writes:

> But the easy, though cruel acquisition of gold, soon rendered the immediate possessors of it neglectful of manufactures and agriculture. Mean while the other nations of Europe, though still excluded from America, were thrown into a ferment by the discovery; so that the riches the Spaniards acquired with so much

ease, obeying the infallible attraction of labour and industry, only passed through their hands in order to circulate in Holland, England, and France.[14]

On one hand Beccaria's text sounds like an elaborate apology for colonialism, a form of racist anthropology that supposes that those nations which have mines will tend to be lazy and unproductive, and require only a productive nation to stir up the native labor force from its torpor. On the other hand, Beccaria expresses a typical symptom of European political economy: mine envy. Raw materials are ambivalent: they bear the danger of anomie.

Various biographical accounts by Beccaria's contemporaries stress a personal mythology of ennui/anomie. In the introduction to his collected works we read: "He was...naturally taciturn and inclined to meditation...This character, which apparently seemed to be stupidity, remained constant for all of his life."[15] After Beccaria achieves fame and is courted by Catherine II of Russia, the imperial court of prince Kaunitz-Ritzberg sends a delegation to convince him to stay in Lombardy, since "consideration given to national individual talents stirs some from lethargy and slumber, and frees some others from despair."[16] Beccaria even participated in his own self-mythologization. For instance, he devised his epitaph to read: "vitam minus ambitiose quam tranquille vixit."

At this intersection of embellished individual biography and national economical history, we find the collapse of anomie and ennui into a single figure. In other words, it is far too easy to psychologize anomie, to make of it an analogue for national or personal lack of desire. Such a slippage, or *lectio facilior,* suppresses the very potentiality of anomie in the sense that Agamben has been developing in his recent work.

Money and Sovereignty

In political economy, the sovereign oversees the minting of coins. His face is stamped on money to guarantee value and fidelity. The sovereign is the king, but also the name of the coin that is stamped under this authority and bears his mark (the sovereign, the crown, and so on). Similarly, it is the sovereign under whose auspices mining takes place. He declares the value of mining, making it his Other. The sovereign is outside of the law (he can declare the value of currency only as he does not engage with it in exchange), but he is also inside the law as he recognizes the value of currency and collects taxes from the people over whom he rules.[17] The sovereign decides on the proportion of gold and silver in any monetary system, just as he guarantees the value of coins.[18] As Marx outlines with great care in The *Grundrisse*, money as a medium of circulation—that is, as coin—loses its value as such. In order to be money, it has to be melted down, or demonetized, it has to shed its merely symbolic value. Coins have national or local characters, but not universal ones. In Marx's terms, "a coin acquires a political title, and talks, as it were, a different language in different countries."[19] When melted down, gold, silver are no longer symbols, but quantities, universal commodities. Money is the negation of the medium of circulation as such, that is, of the coin; but it contains the potential to be turned into coin. Money inhabits a realm of anomie. As money it has value only as gold and silver, but the face that the state impresses on it has no importance.

If we extend the logic of money and acknowledge the Sovereign as "he who decides on the state of exception," then he is the Other of monetary indeterminacy.[20] He could be defined as non-float, as non-materialization of wealth. And in the contemporary world, he is no longer embodied in a single figure, but has become convention, but for that "he" has not lost his qualities as Sovereign.

The thinker who offers the most lucid meditation on the relation of money, sovereignty and anomie is Ernest Kantorowicz. In that classic of political theology, *The King's Two Bodies,* we learn that the possessions of the demesne are unalienable, existing in a state of anomie. Roman and canon law give rise to the concept of a fisc that never dies. In the Middle Ages, taxation was ad hoc, *casus necessitatis*, and evoked in states of emergency. Over time, however, taxes are levied annually, *necessitas regis et regni,* even if the fiction of an unrepeatable event or emergency persists in monetary rhetoric. In other words, taxation undergoes a genealogy such that the state of exception becomes permanent.

According to Agamben, however, Kantorowicz undervalues the precedent of Roman law as embedded in English monarchic law.[21] That is, the king's two bodies should be understood in relation to the distinct Roman concepts of *potestas* and *auctoritas,* not just the office of the sovereign—the fisc that never dies—but the actual person. This principle extends also to Mussolini and Hitler. While these figures do hold the respective offices as heads of government (*potestas*), their peculiar power also comes from their bodies, so that they "belong to the biopolitical tradition of *auctoritas* and not the juridical one of *potestas.*"[22] These leaders exercise extraordinary powers of personal charisma, and they are not substitutable with just any other persona. The implications of this for the state of exception are crucial: "The norm [of law, of the judicial] can be applied to the normal situation and can be suspended without totally annulling the juridical order because in the form of *auctoritas,* or sovereign decision, it refers immediately to life, it springs from life."[23] It is because of the biopolitical nature of the leader as *auctor,* in all of its specificity, deriving from Roman law, that the sovereign decision functions as a state of exception.

Representing the Market

Let us consider, then, two representation of the market that may help us think about the applicability of the "state of exception" and the sovereign decision in the monetary realm. Antonioni's remarkable film *Eclipse* was released in 1962, toward the end of the economy boom of postwar Italy. The film opens with the breakup of a love affair, particularly painful because of the lack of any clear temporal or spatial boundaries. There is no law, no definitive marker, as Antonioni makes eminently clear through his slow-paced editing, shot selection, and minimal dialogue. Rather, the characters inhabit an anomic zone of indeterminacy where they are neither together nor apart.

Following this excruciating scene shot on location in EUR, we follow Vittoria (Monica Vitti) into the Rome stock exchange. She is looking for her mother, who, as an "individual investor" (and, probably, as a woman) remains excluded from the center of a series of concentric circles with progressively limited access. Indeed, the entire exchange is decentered inasmuch as the real market is in Milan (reached by analogue telephone), or better, in the United States. Rome is just a satellite market, and its marginality is crucial to the scene in question.

Vittoria's mother is quite preoccupied with a potential crisis in the market and she has no time for her daughter. Rather, just as Vittoria attempts to speak with her mother, a bell rings loudly, signaling a moment of silence for a dead colleague, "like for soccer players," as a broker, Riccardo, (Alain Delon), notes. Vittoria and Riccardo stand behind marble pillars, waiting for "time to resume." Phones keep ringing, as if to emphasize that this "pause" is local to the Rome exchange and Milan isn't even aware of it. In the pre-digital Roman market, price changes are reflected on a large board. There is a moment of blankness as the (automated) numbers flip over: one of several eclipses in the film, just like the clock suspended from the ceiling. In the digital world it is impossible to represent, filmically, the shift from one interval of time to another, the moment of transition when a stock rises or falls or price.

At the center—what should logically be the motor of the market—is a public address system that looks remarkably like an old-fashioned accountants' lamp. The technology of this market seems nostalgic, perhaps for an era of face-to-face exchange. Antonioni makes it eminently clear that time does not stop during this full minute of on-screen time. In fact, the (nostalgic) center of the market is the place of the enunciation of death. This pre-post Fordist scene proves with remarkable foresight that the market is a perpetual motion machine that exists in a spatial and temporal no-man's-land, a state of exception; a state of emergency that has become the norm.

The moment of silence in *Eclipse* is eerily echoed in a second scene, not from a film, but from "real life" (as broadcast on cable television or streaming on the Internet). The scene takes place at 9 a.m. on September 17th, 2001, as Wall Street wakes up and reopens for business after 9/11. Traders crowd the floor of the exchange, filled with apparent anticipation. On the mezzanine above, a group of dignitaries stands with grave faces. A bell rings to signal a minute of silence, just as in Antonioni's film. And as in the film, the camera pans over the bodies of the traders, making clear through micro-movements, nervous ticks, coughs, phones, computers buzzing—the soundscape of the infosphere—that time never stops. Some people shed tears. The silence is followed by an *a cappella* rendition of "God Bless America." More shuffling, tears, buzzing. Finally, a fire captain representing the "heroes of 9/11" rings the opening bell. A collective exhalation is followed by the usual frantic movements. The herd had been trained during the week prior to think that buying was a sign of patriotism, a gesture of defiance against the terrorists. The market rebooting itself is the ultimate ritual of the permanence of "our way of life." The scene stages an end of the state of emergency, a return to law.

In the new economy, "old wealth" or "blue chip" companies from a fantasized past actually manufactured things. That is, the brand name appeared on a building that was also the factory or plant. Now we realize that what the developed world can best focus on are value-added elements such as design and marketing, and therefore the actual production of goods is outsourced to subcontractors or EMSs (Electronic Manufacturing Services). These factories, as Naomi Klein has described them in depth in *No Logo* are, of course, known for their flexibility and low costs. They exist in non-spaces (enterprise zones that exist as places only in a dematerialized sense) and in non-times (work goes on constantly, without any break, and thus does not correspond to the lived time of human beings).

When people purchase securities today, they most often do so not using actual currency, but paying electronically or transferring funds. At times these funds exist in a non-state of suspension known as "the float," but then they reappear, rematerialize, as it were. And even if the money exchanged never actually falls into the hands of traders as paper, even if traders never receive those engraved and ornate paper products known as stock certificates, it would seem that the emergence from the float, the electronic confirmation of the arrival of funds or the closing of a transaction could properly be called a rematerialization. Even quarterly reports are now offered electronically. So the entire transaction, from idea, research, buying, to owning, and eventually selling, is potentially dematerialized. Equities trading involves very little actual contact between human beings, and whatever face-to-face contact there is, it is of a fleeting nature. This goes to explaining why the markets have done as much as they can to present a materialized image that will make people feel comfortable. The bull and the bear serve as totemic symbols of markets. Markets have bells rung by celebrities to signal the human presence on the floor. The mass of paper that is left to clean up after a day's trading seems a necessary byproduct. The Nasdaq set up shop in Herald Square, literally in a store front that has nothing behind it, a "floorless" and fully digitized market. Reporters are said to be broadcasting live from the "Nasdaq market *site*." The word "site" must be included since there is no market and indeed trades are done by a series of computers located miles away. In the background behind reporters, symbols and numbers scroll across hyper-modern screens. This is a nostalgic referent to an older form of exchange, a mere pointer to a site, but not a place that a human being could inhabit since it is space with no depth, only a consumer window out onto the world, a reflection.

Pure violence, money, anomie

I have already expressed a certain skepticism toward the enterprise of using Agamben's work to think about a realm beyond law. Having said this, the "state of exception" remains a highly attractive concept for thinking about the complex interrelations of time, space, money, anomie; about personal (psychological) and national (in)action. Moreover, the law (of the state, the camps, and so on) could and should be thought in relation to money (law of the market). It is difficult to resist an easy fall into a psychology of ambiguity (the gray zone). Leaving aside the rather significant economic developments that separate Rome's quaint exchange of the cold war era to the new economy market at the dawn of the war on terror, both scenes mentioned above represent—each in its own fictive manner—the state of exception as it pertains to the market.[24] Like the circles that Agamben reproduces in *Homo Sacer,* the circles of the market contain what is not ex-cepted (ex-capere), that which is sovereign. But as in Agamben's work, these scenes suggest a certain violence and fear. It is precisely in acting as a market-maker that the multitude becomes a community, just as the multitude becomes a people through the recognition of a sovereign, an action, that is itself potentially, purely, violent.[25]

CHAPTER TWO

PAOLO MATTEUCCI

SOVEREIGNTY, BORDERS, EXCEPTION

Elaborating on Giorgio Agamben's arguments, according to which, "faced with the unstoppable progression of what has been called a 'global civil war,' the state of exception tends increasingly to appear as the dominant paradigm of government in contemporary politics,"[26] several intellectuals have analyzed the unfolding of the exception in the present geo-political scenario with the purpose of criticizing the most aberrant manifestations of contemporary politics, namely detention camps.[27] While much has been made of the fact that contemporary camps, such as Guantánamo, appear to be zones of "suspension of the law" and that their existence is often justified in the name of emergency, an object of even more vehement criticism has been the fact that the camps are physically enclosed by a set of impenetrable borders and thus what happens within them ultimately remains unknown to the general public.

The problem of how to deal with the borders of the exception is not absent from Agamben's writings. For instance, the opening pages of *State of Exception* suggest that, in elaborating a theory of the exception,

> The question of borders becomes all the more urgent: if exceptional measures are the result of periods of political crisis and, as such, must be understood on political and not juridico-constitutional grounds, then they find themselves in the paradoxical position of being juridical measures that cannot be understood in legal terms, and the state of exception appears as the legal form of what cannot have legal form.[28]

Agamben's allusion to the "question of borders" is not followed, however, by immediate clarification. It is specifically for this reason, I maintain, that it seems to disclose several heuristic points of departure. Agamben does not tell us, for example, if the most immediate concern should be to identify the limits that belong to the theory of the exception, or if it is more urgent that we ask whether or not (and in which ways) the category of "borders" can be applied to the state of exception. Since the state of exception is "neither external nor internal to the juridical order,"[29] I believe it is also crucial to consider the possibility that one should conceive not only the exception, but also its "borders," in terms of ambivalence, that is to say neither inside nor outside their juridical, political, or spatio-temporal dimensions.[30]

In the following pages, I will try to intervene on the current debate concerning the limits and borders of the exception. First, I argue that the relationship between norm and exception cannot be understood as a binary opposition because there is no such a thing as a boundary-line that separates the two. Second, I propose that in approaching the relation between exception and norm we need to abandon (or, at the very least, radically re-conceptualize) the notion of boundary in favour of an understanding of the border as a zone of topological indeterminacy and indistinguishableness. Eventually, it is my aim to call attention to the contradictory nature (if not the danger) of the attempts made, in the name of the "solemn invocations of the 'sacred and inalienable' rights of man,"[31] to delimit the unfolding of the exception into a set of clear-cut boundaries.

To support my claims, I will make a move inspired by the work of Giorgio Agamben. In attempting "to untangle the *aporias*"[32] of the modern theory of the exception, Agamben focuses on the *iustitium* and demonstrates how, by representing an "archetype of the modern *Ausnahmezustand,*"[33] this Roman institution informs contemporary paradigms of governmental politics. In this essay, I propose to discuss an urgent problem in contemporary sovereignty (the "question of borders") through an analysis of the depiction provided by Roman historiography of the *terminus.* Like *iustitium,* not only does the Roman *terminus* seem not "to have been given sufficient attention by legal historians and theorists of public law,"[34] but it also provides us with "a miniature model"[35] that illuminates, from a contemporary perspective, the topographic relationship between sovereignty and exception.

In Latin, *terminus* has three principal meanings. All three seem to be inherently related to the problem that Henri Lefebvre has called "the production of space."[36] The term indicates: (1) a series of material landmarks used to delimit the territories under the control of Rome; (2) a divinity existing on the Capitoline before and after the arrival of Jupiter on the hill; (3) a physical stone which was left inside the temple dedicated to *Iuppiter Optimus Maximus* at the moment of its construction. Whether taken into consideration separately or analyzed together, all three meanings of *terminus* reveal that, topologically, the exception is indistinguishable from the norm.[37]

In its first meaning, the Latin *terminus* designates any physical instrument used to mark the border of a given portion of land. Typically in the forms of *cippus*, *saxum*, or *miliarium,* the Roman *terminus* appears as an active producer of space that simultaneously performs processes of territorial definition and spatial partition. On the one hand, in marking the end (or the *finis*) of a territory, *terminus* functioned as a means of delimitation of the land. On the other hand, in dividing two or more pieces of territory, *terminus* also performed a process of separation. The *termini* separated the *urbs* from the *pomerium,* the sacred and the profane spaces, the city from the country, and the territories of the Empire from the rest of the world.[38]

As Giulia Piccaluga has demonstrated in a fundamental study published in 1974 and entitled *Terminus: I segni di confine nella religione romana,* it is crucial to understand that the Latin *termini* were not used to measure territorial extension, and they did not indicate geographical or cosmic coordinates.[39] Other means, the *limiti* for example, were used for these purposes. The *termini* instead constituted, in Piccaluga's words, "particular sacral means through which it was possible to exercise control over several aspects of reality."[40]

Furthermore—and here we can observe the first valence of *terminus* as a *dispositif* of exception—the *termini* were not considered to be part of the territories to which they referred. The *termini* represented, as Piccaluga has argued, "external points" with respect to the field of which they delimited the extension.[41]

By viewing this feature of *termini* in light of Carl Schmitt's statement according to which "the 'ordering of the space' that is...constitutive of the sovereign *nomos* is...not only a 'taking of land' (*Landesnahme*)—the determination of a juridical and a territorial ordering (of an *Ordnung* and an *Ortung*)—but above all a 'taking of the outside,' an exception (*Ausnahme*)," [42] it is possible to understand the Roman *terminus,* in this first sense, as a topological projection of the exception. Marking the border of a given extension of land, but not being part of the territory it refers to, *terminus* seems to spatially represent that point at which "in order to apply a norm it is ultimately necessary to suspend its application."[43]

Incidentally, beginning with the reign of Numa Pompilius, Roman law severely punished those who moved or removed the *termini.* Any person found guilty of having displaced a *terminus* was, often alongside with his oxen, declared *sacer.* Anyone could kill such a person and not be considered a murderer.[44]

The *termini,* as Ovid explains in the *Fasti,* were also objects of worship and the sacrificial feast of the *Terminalia* was dedicated to them.[45] While each boundary marker was given its own *numen,* all *termini* were considered the simultaneous expression of a single deity: the god Terminus who resided with Jupiter on the *capitolium.*[46]

Also in this second meaning—that is to say, as a deity—*terminus* appears to be related strictly to the notion of the exception. In order to fully grasp this relationship, it is necessary to look at how *terminus,* ambivalently located both on the *capitolium* and in each boundary mark, is depicted in Roman historiography. According to several authors, before work could begin on Jupiter's temple on the *capitolium,* it was necessary to interpellate the *augures.* On the old Capitoline, in fact, several sacred buildings dedicated to a series of deities had to be exaugurated in order to make room for the temple of Jupiter. When asked to express their approval of being moved out, the divinities of the *capitolium* agreed to leave with only one exception: Terminus.[47]

The moment of Terminus' refusal, as Piccaluga has suggested, constitutes a crucial episode in the affirmation of the sovereign order brought by Jupiter. In introducing an element of ultimate "otherness" in the territories of Jupiter's sovereignty, Terminus allows Jupiter to affirm his own sovereign power and "to sustain the whole reality." Thanks to its immovability, for Piccaluga, Terminus functions as the guarantor of the "indestructibility of the *capitolium.*"[48]

It is important to highlight the fact that, according to Roman historiography, no punishment followed Terminus' refusal. It is therefore problematic to interpret Terminus' in-exaugurability as a simple act of transgression of the norm. Rather, recalling Agamben's statement that, in the state of exception, the "application is suspended, but the law, as such, remains in force,"[49] it is possible to see Terminus' refusal as an archetypal moment of exception. At the moment of Jupiter's arrival on the *capitolium,* it seems, "what cannot be included in any way is included in the form of the exception."[50]

Incidentally, the feast of the *Terminalia* also seems to represent, this time in the temporal dimension, the insertion of an anomic element into the constituted order. The *Terminalia* was held every year on the 23rd day of February, at the "end" of the Roman solar-lunar year. It inaugurated a period of five days named *regifugium,* during which the *rex sacrorum* was required to leave the city in order to "demonstrate to the Roman people assembled in the *comitium* that there was no more a king to qualify and define the organization of time."[51] The anomic period of the *regifugium,* that Brelich and Sabbatucci have respectively defined as "a sort of temporal *no man's land*"[52] and "a no-one's time,"[53] continued until the appearance of the new moon, at which point the *pontifex* recalled the *rex sacrorum* into the *comitium* so that he could declare the beginning of the first month on the new year.[54]

In Roman historiography, *terminus* also held a third meaning. It referred to an actual stone, called *Terminus,* located in the *Cella Iovis* inside the temple of *Iuppiter Optimus Maximus Capitolinus.* Today, to my knowledge, there is no available iconographic representation of this stone, but we know from Virgil and Lactantius that it was considered "immobile" and "shapeless."[55] We also know that a *foramen* (a hole) was left above the stone in the temple's roof. In this way, *Terminus* could remain directly exposed to the open space of the cosmos.[56]

In its third meaning, the Latin *terminus* also seems to constitute a spatial projection of the state of exception. Simultaneously closed up inside the temple and exposed to the open space of the cosmos, *Terminus* does not appear to be properly located "outside" Jupiter's law, but it is rather, to use Agamben's words, "exposed and threatened"[57] on "a threshold, or a zone of indifference, where inside and outside do not exclude each other but rather blur with each other."[58] The English translation of Agamben's words (according to which inside and outside "blur with each other"), unfortunately, does not fully capture the meaning of the original Italian, which reads: "dentro e fuori non si escludono, ma s'inde*terminano*" (emphasis added).[59]

In being simultaneously internal and external, essential and extraneous to sovereign space, the *terminus,* in all three of its meanings, seems to offer a topographic representation of the "relation of exception" described by Agamben in the first section of *Homo Sacer.* As the text states,[60]

> If one wanted to represent schematically the relation between the state of nature and the state of law that takes shape in the state of exception, one could have recourse to two circles that at first appear to be distinct (Fig. 1) but later, in the state of exception, show themselves to be in fact inside each other (Fig. 2). When the exception starts to become the rule, the two circles coincide in absolute indistinction (Fig. 3).

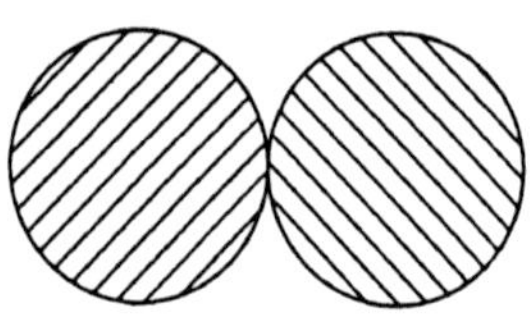

Figure 1

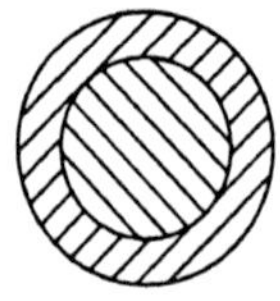

Figure 2

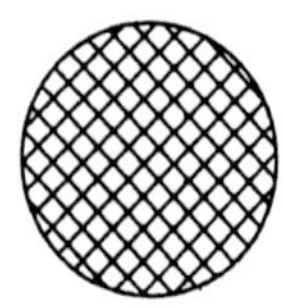

Figure 3

In reading this schema, it is important to keep in mind that *terminus* was located at the center of Rome (in the *Cella Iovis* of the temple of *Iuppiter Maximus* on the *capitolium*) as well as disseminated throughout the Roman territories (when used as a means of delimitation and separation of different properties) and placed at the ultimate geographical limits of Roman sovereignty (as in the case of the *termini publici* that separated the Roman territories from the rest of the world).[61]

The inner circle represented in Figure 2, which we can read in relation to the in-exaugurability of the Terminus of the *capitolium,* contains in itself the potentiality to extend itself to the end frontiers of sovereignty—here represented by the external circle. At the same time, with its dissemination inside and throughout Rome's territories, *terminus* also embodies the condition of indistinctness and indetermination relating sovereignty and exception as represented in Figure 3.

The relationship between *terminus* and *Iuppiter* demonstrates how, in scrutinizing the complex relationship between sovereignty and exception, it seems necessary to first assess the reciprocal indeterminacy that characterizes the two terms. Secondly, reading *terminus* as a topographical model for the relation of exception seems to advance the possibility that, in addressing the contemporary unfolding of the exception, the notion of the boundary-line should perhaps be abandoned. It is useful to recall here that, for Agamben, "the originary relation of law to life is not application but Abandonment."[62] Furthermore, as Agamben claims in *Homo Sacer* when discussing "the camp as a bio-political paradigm of the modern," the space of exception is

> Placed outside the normal juridical order, but it is nevertheless not simply an external space. What is included … is, according to the etymological sense of the term 'exception' (*ex-capere*), *taken outside,* included through its own exclusion. But what is first of all taken into the juridical order is the state of exception itself.[63]

The topographical model represented by *terminus* seems also to support the hypothesis that, from a contemporary perspective, it is urgent that we do not formulate and identify the series of (juridical, political, temporal, or spatial) limits belonging to the emergency and the exception, and instead accept the possibility that contemporary sovereignty has abandoned traditional notions of border in favour of spatial indeterminacy and indistinguishability.

In conclusion, I propose that in the future we do not follow the theoretical approaches that attempt to formulate a set of limits and borders with which to frame the unfolding of the exception. Rather than calling for the re-inscription of Guantánamo into the norms of the Geneva Convention, and rather than making an appeal to the "universal rights to humane treatment," I propose that we instead concern ourselves with the past and present continuities between dictatorship and democracy.

CHAPTER THREE

ANDREA BENINO

FROM *STATO-PIANO* TO *STATO-CRISI*: PROLETARIAN SELF-VALORIZATION AND THE STATE OF EXCEPTION

This paper analyzes three works written by Antonio Negri during the 1970s: "Partito operaio contro il lavoro" (1973), "Proletari e Stato" (1975), and "Il dominio e il sabotaggio" (1977). It argues that, in these works, Negri formulates a militant account of how a political subject can be seen as a product of what Alain Badiou has called a "procedure of truth." The essay also attempts to demonstrate the contemporary importance of Negri's analysis by relating it to Giorgio Agamben's reflections on biopolitics and the state of exception.

Negri's works belong to the tradition of *operaismo,* a current in Italian Marxism that identifies labor struggle as the driving force of capitalist development. One of the central documents of *operaismo* is Mario Tronti's collection of essays *Operai e capitale.* In one of the essays collected in that book, "Lenin in Inghilterra," Tronti demands a reversal of the traditional view according to which labor struggles follow capitalist development.[64] Tronti argues that when capital has reached a degree of socialization corresponding to what Marx calls the "real subsumption of labor under capital," labor struggles become productive: capital can only react to these struggles by finding ways of instrumentalizing the demands advanced in them.[65] In the words of Tronti: "Once capital has developed on a social scale, capitalist development is subordinate to labor struggles; it follows them and must make the political mechanism of its production process correspond to them."[66] Within this theoretical framework, Marx's *Grundrisse* becomes a privileged reference point. Marx's concepts of a "general intellect" and of the "social individual" are treated as a theoretical anticipation of mature capitalism and used to explore labor subjectivity.

In the works to be examined here, Negri invokes Marx's discussion of the tendential decline of the average profit rate, using this discussion to explore the transformations of Italian capitalism that resulted from the labor struggles of the

1970s. In the *Grundrisse,* Marx says the average profit rate depends on the relation between the part of capital exchanged for living labour and the part existing in the form of raw material and means of production. Hence, the smaller the portion exchanged for living labour becomes, the smaller becomes the rate of profit.[67] According to Negri, the decline of the profit rate, a mere tendency in Marx, had become a reality in the Italy of the 1970s, due to capital's failure to recruit living labor for the production process. Society itself—the bodies and minds of the persons from which the social network is composed—had become the main basis for capitalist valorization; consequently, direct labor was no longer the principal source of wealth. The determination of value by abstract unities of labor time had become problematic; the law of value, the fundamental law of capitalist valorization, no longer functioned. Labor struggles had begun to dramatically infringe on capital's possibilities for valorization; the dialectic of labor struggles and capital had imposed a limit on the exploitation of living labor by forcing capital to complete the process of socialization. This limit consisted in the refusal of workers to provide capital with their labor force. The crisis of the law of value revealed the catastrophic effect of the insurgence of labor subjectivity on the strategy of capital.

Negri's analysis recognises in the *operaio massa,* the worker of the Fordist factory, the force that compels capital to engage in a project of massive restructuring, a project that coincides with the complete socialization of capital and consequently with the expansion of the struggle: from the factory to the whole of society. A new subject of exploitation is constituted, the *operaio sociale,* bearer of new forms of conflict, a subject as radical as it is widely disseminated across the social field. As Negri says: "*the category of the 'working class' goes into crisis, but as the proletariat it continues to produce all the effects that proper to it on te social terrain as a whole.*"[68] It is precisely in the category of the operaio sociale, or of the socialized proletariat, that Negri identifies the revolutionary subject of the new struggles.

Applying certain categories from Alain Badiou's work to this analysis, one can interpret the rise of the socialized proletariat as the (political, cultural, and economic) crisis of the "situation" constituted by the Italian society of the 1970s. Direct labor, the category on which the struggle of the socialized proletariat is founded (that is, the ontological basis for the struggle against capitalist exploitation), can be interpreted as the "void" that refuses to be integrated into the Italian "situtation."

In *L'être et l'événement,* Badiou invokes set theory to develop a political ontology in which the "situation" is defined as a structured multiplicity whose elements are treated as unitary, measurable, and stable (as elements of a given set), in accordance with the regulative principle "count-as-one." Crucially, the elements that belong to a situation are, ontologically speaking, a multiplicity of multiplicities: that is, a phenomenon that ultimately transcends measure and can be represented only if has been "captured." The elements of a situation only exist (as elements) by means of the "count-as-one" that structures the situation by reducing the immeasurable to the measurable.

The ontological category at the centre of Negri's analysis of the Italian insurgence, that of living labor as a radically indeterminate productive capacity, corresponds precisely to that which escapes the regulative mechanisms of the situation in Badiou's model. When production has been completely socialized and the law of value no longer functions, labor becomes the void that sends the situation that is Italian capitalism into crisis, defying that situation's regulative principle (its mechanisms of measure). Yet the identification of this void is possibile only from within, by means of a militant praxis, capable of finding a proper name for the subject risen from the void, the subject that cannot be represented in the situation.

This theoretical model allows one to conceptualize the Italian insurgence of the 1970s without recourse to the notion of a political subject that pre-exists the struggles and directs them from outside. The subject of which Negri speaks, and which can be named "socialized proletariat struggling for self-valorization," is not defined in terms of socio-economic or psychological characteristics; its character is strictly political.[69] Negri's proletariat is a subject that constitutes itself within the struggle, subjectivizing itself in the void that sends the given situation—the Italian State as a juridical, economic, and political system—into crisis. The so-called *Libri del rogo* (Negri's political interventions from the 1970s) do not describe a sociological class, but speak from within the space opened by political struggle; they give a subject a proper name. No analysis can deduce the insurgence of the socialized proletariat struggling for self-valorization from the situation, but once the process of subjectivization has begun, to live within this process is to give a name to the subject, to determine its characteristics, given the basis of the specific dynamic of the process. This means that a political praxis can be verified only from within the praxis itself. What is more, if every politics is situated, it must necessarily reach a point where it exhausts the process of subjectivization that made it possible. There is an important implication: namely, that it is not helpful to think about a political praxis in terms of failure or defeat. If it is possible to identify, a posteriori and from a theoretical point of view, certain flaws within the texts that were part of the political space constituted by the appearance of the void within the situation, those texts are nonetheless characterized by a "sense of truth" that follows from their participation in what Badiou calls the event, the catastrophic collapse of the situation in the face of the void.

The merit of the political interventions by Negri to be examined here consists in their having participated in the catastrophe suffered by the Italian situation of the 1970s. By means of this participation, Negri's interventions succeeded in putting into practice a procedure of truth. The fact that such participation was made possible by the appearance of a new subjectivity is the only criterium by which this new procedure of truth can be verified. The new subjectivity constituted itself in the struggle for self-valorization, a struggle both for the destruction of the capitalist system of valorization and for the affirmation of a wealth understood in ontological terms. As Negri says, "Proletarian self-valorization is the strength [forza] to withdraw from exchange value and the capacity to base itself on use values."[70] In other words, self-valorization is subtraction from the abstract measure of wage labor and expansion of the productive capacities shared by the men and women unified in struggle. In his texts from the 1970s, Negri proceeds from politico-economic analysis (the crisis of Italian capitalism demonstrated by its irreversible decline in profit) to the politico-ontological level (the concept of self-valorization). It is therefore no accident that the ontological dimension of Marx's thought is emphatically emphasized in the lectures on the *Grundrisse* that Negri held in Paris in 1978; the properly philosophical character of Negri's political writings emerges from this peculiar counterpoint of praxis and theory. In Negri's fourth lecture on the *Grundrisse*, devoted to the concepts of surplus labor and exploitation, we can see clearly what the opposition between proletarian use value and capitalist exchange value means: capital and labor are two forces whose fundamental antagonism becomes progressively more explicit with the socialization of both production and struggle. It is in these pages that the theme of labor as subjectivity—that is, as pure potentiality—is first addressed.[71] Labor, in the sense of an absolutely indeterminate creative capacity, is not simply something objective; rather, its existence is necessarily subjective (that is, the creative capacity is necessarily embodied). When labor is understood in these terms, there emerges an irreducible antagonism between labor and capitalist exploitation: the indeterminacy of labor as creative capacity creates endless difficulties for capital, which can prosper only by objectivizing—and hence measuring—that which is purely subjective. From the point of view of the revolution, the subjective character of labor constitutes a kind of ultimate wealth: that of a creative capacity that escapes capitalism's mechanisms of measure, and which opposes itself to those mechanisms as production assumes an increasingly socialized character. Capital follows the development of labor struggles, recuperating them by means of economic restructuring and modernization, but it eventually loses its positive function; the political insurgence of proletarian use value and the subtraction of labor's creative capacity, from the mechanisms of measure, constitute the final limit to capitalist command, the point where that command: loses its progressive aura and exposes itself as a violent imposition of the law of value on all of society. The ontological substratum identified by Negri in proletarian use value, the true basis for self-valorization, escapes the situation constituted by the capitalist mode of production; labor subjectivity defies measure and hence refuses to be incorporated into the situation governed by the regulative principles of capitalism. To ground oneself in use value is, therefore, to subjectivize oneself in the struggle against capitalist exploitation, to open oneself to a dimension that sends exploitation into crisis.

Until now, we have considered the emergence of a new subjectivity and its "catastrophic" effects on the Italian capitalist structure of the 1970s. Badiou's theoretical model also requires us to emphasize that the the main task of every situational structure is that of completely abolishing the void, or of eliminating the possibility of catastrophe by imposing the regulative principle "count-as-one" on every element of the structure. This task remains fundamental even if it is never fully achieved. In *Libri del rogo,* Negri identifies the imposition of a regime of permanent crisis as Italian capitalism's response to the new political subjectivity that emerged from the struggles of the 1970s. Italian capitalism defended itself by imposing a state of exception. Historical evidence for the truth of this claim can be found in the anti-terrorism laws that were passed by decree during the 1970s. The so-called *leggi speciali* need to be understood in terms of a state of emergency characterized by the suspension of democratic legal protocol.[72] One of the most striking examples of the Italian state's campaign of repression is the so-called "April 7th trial."[73] From April 7, 1979 onward, several hundred militants were arrested and incarcerated, heralding the "beginning of the end" for Italy's social protest movements. According to the *teorema Calogero*, by which the entire operation was justified, *Autonomia Operaia* (the vast revolutionary movement that spread through the country from the mid-1970s onward) was closely linked to the various groups then engaging in "armed struggle."[74] According to the charges, the leaders of *Autonomia* were the secret masterminds or *cervelli occulti* not just of Autonomia, but also of the Red Brigades and other armed, clandestine organizations. After a series of protracted trials and many years of preventive detention, the *teorema* revealed itself to be unfounded.

According to the *teorema Calogero,* Antonio Negri was one of the higher echelons of the fictitious super-organization postulated during the trial; several of his books were used as evidence by the prosecution.[75] Negri's publisher Feltrinelli destroyed its stocks of these books, attempting to prevent Negri's written statements from becoming an object of public debate and demonstrating how legal and police repression could find unexpected allies in the sphere of culture.

On the basis of this history, one can trace in the *Libri del rogo* a theory of juridical exceptionalism. When read in the light of Giorgio Agamben's recent studies on the topic, this theory promises to reveal those aspects of Negri's political interventions that are perhaps most theoretically relevant for us today.

Giorgio Agamben has devoted himself to a structural analysis of the state of exception, defining it as that practical and theoretical mechanism or *dispositif* which, in separating the norm from its application, "introduces a zone of anomie into the law in order to make the effective regulation of the real possible."[76] The state of exception is a suspension of conventional legal protocol intended to assure a more complete application of the juridical norm. One can say that, in the Italy of the 1970s, capital responded to the radicality of the class struggle by implementing such a state of exception. In fact, according to Negri, "the collapse of the law of value, which is the law of market freedom and the functional horizon of refomist planning, deprives the action of total capital—in the form of the State—of every rationale for command other than violence."[77] In this view, the state is a mere instrument of capital; it is the preferred means for guaranteeing the survival of capital and its control over living labor. Juridical exceptionalism (the state of emergency or state of exception) is a political tool; indeed, it is the only device available to a capitalist order that has lost every innovative capacity, a capitalist order that imposes itself as exploitation of the creative capacity of society itself.

At the level of development achieved by Italian capitalism, class struggle becomes an immediately political struggle against the state and its articulations, which are simply instruments of rule, devices for exercising command over production. Every semblance of democracy and legality is abandoned; the mystified concepts of civil society, as the place where a mediation between class interests can occur, and of the state, as the neutral space in which these interests can be expressed, are both abandoned when the state explicitly assumes the tasks of control and domination. The Italian condition is of a country torn by a form of civil war: two opposed factions conduct their struggle outside the terrain of legality, and outside the dialectic of democracy on which legality is based. On one side there is the crisis state as a manifestation of capitalist subjectivity; on the other, there is proletarian subjectivity. In fact, it is this proletarian subjectivity that eliminates both the possibility of capitalist planning, of a compromise between struggle and development, and the law of value. The political project that Negri formulates on the basis of this analysis is that of constructing a party; this party must not, however, be thought of in terms of representation, and neither in Leninist terms, as a separate vanguard. The function of the party as conceptualized by Negri is to concentrate the aggressive force that proletarian practices, such as re-appropriation and the refusal of work, have disseminated across the social field. The party gives unity and direction to the diffuse forms of proletarian counterpower, a counterpower whose appearance corresponds to the constitution of an antagonistic subjectivity that does not merely respond to capitalist re-structuring, but acts autonomously.[78]

This radical and irreducible dualism between crisis state and socialized proletariat governs the theoretical space within which Negri formulates his analysis. What is the link between this analysis and Agamben's theories of biopolitics and the state of exception? In *Homo sacer,* Agamben invokes Badiou's *L'être et l'événement*, defining the exception as that which "*cannot be included in the whole of which it is a member and cannot be a member of the whole in which it is always already included.*"[79] This definition offers a perfect description of the condition of living labor as it was in the struggling class described by Negri. Living labor's indeterminate productive capacity is included in capitalism's productive structure via the mediation of money; this transaction, on which capitalism is founded, only becomes possible by an equally fundamental exclusion—living labor is "captured" within capitalism's productive structure by its very exclusion.

It is worth noting the extent to which this analysis converges with Agamben's analytic of power, according to which politics is based on the simultaneous exclusion and "capture" of bare life.[80] The state of exception—that is, the application of a rule by means of its suspension—demonstrates how a norm can only establish its object of reference by presupposing something that remains outside the referential relation. Paradoxically, the norm must also establish a relation to that which is excluded—a relation of exclusion. This is what Agamben terms inclusive exclusion. The case of the *homo sacer* (the man who can be killed by anyone without legal consequences, but who must not be sacrificed, and who is therefore simultaneously excluded from civil and from divine law) provides the archetypal example of inclusive exclusion: "*homo sacer* names something like the originary "political" relation, which is to say, bare life insofar as it operates in an inclusive exclusion as the referent of the sovereign decision."[81] Agamben's work seems to imply that bare life, the ontological substratum that has always already been captured within the structure of sovereign power, can never provide a solid foundation for a truly revolutionary politics. This would seem to be the meaning of the various criticisms of Marxism formulated by Agamben in *Homo sacer*. Agamben argues that Marxism fails to recognize the basic structure of sovereign power, such that it risks resembling the enemy it sets out to combat.[82] While the works by Negri discussed above are part of a Marxist discourse and share its limitations, one can nonetheless say that one of their fundamental theoretical aims consists in formulating an internal critique of Marxism, forcing it to confront one of its blind spots: the fundamental link between bare life and sovereign power.

On the one hand, Negri's ontological conceptualization of the socialized worker, or of bare life as an absolutely indeterminate labor force, reveals the limit of Marxism with regard to the biopolitical character of power and sovereignty. On the other hand, the concept of the party, or the radically dualist conceptualization of counterpower, retreats from this threshold in order to fall back into an essentially juridical notion of power, a notion that sees in power no more than a capacity for repression.

By identifying the crisis state as the threshold of Italian capitalism in its modern form, beyond which the exception becomes the rule and bare life becomes the object of politics, Negri alludes to a situation in which Marxism must be taken beyond its own limits. It seems to me, therefore, that the works by Negri examined here are more than simply an important reference point for understanding Negri's own development as a thinker; they also provide essential tools for understanding, imagining, and conducting the struggles that emerge the new forms of domination today.

CHAPTER FOUR

MAURIZIO VITO

LA MORTE COME PENA: LAW, DEATH PENALTY AND STATE OF EXCEPTION

Il diritto penale…fra tutte le materie è quella
che risente più delle altre del momento politico.
—Italo Mereu

My paper deals with a peculiar form of the "state of exception," namely the one that came to light with the death penalty, when this punishment first appeared in Italy during the Middle Ages. In his book *La morte come pena: Saggio sulla violenza legale,* Italo Mereu analyzes the main reasons that led to its introduction into the Italian penal system up to the moment in which, some six centuries later, it was banned. The point I will make is that a state punishment, such as the death penalty is possible only if the law opens up a space that has been defined as a "state of exception," which is "a borderline concept."[83] That the space at issue inherently belongs to law, or is opened by law, is an argument I will discuss as well. Vagueness or indefiniteness, makes these topics interesting to be examined and, at the same time, hard to firmly pinpoint. In order to grasp better these concepts, I have decided to first follow roughly the historical description of the death penalty Mereu provides in his work, and then to accompany it with theoretical and critical analyses. If my assumption is correct, at the end of my paper the reader will have a clearer idea of the intangible state of exception mentioned above.

To begin with, I would like to recall what Mereu states about the medieval, and therefore, as common sense maintains, barbarian, penal code. First of all he asks in which part of the Middle Ages the death penalty was introduced as a legal punishment: "It is a fact that all along the 'German' or 'Barbarian' Middle Ages…that is the so-called 'dark and deep early Middle Ages', the death penalty does not punish homicide. *Guidrigildo* is used instead."[84] The *guidrigildo* was an amount of money supposed to restore the damage that the culprit had caused. Albeit inadequate and highly arguable, the *guidrigildo* was many steps ahead, as far as the humanity of punishment is concerned, the death penalty, or, say, the *Lex Talionis,* in acknowledging the worthiness of life. Surprisingly enough (or perhaps not), the Sacred Scriptures and the Roman law, according to nineteenth century scholar Antonio Pertile, team up to change this state of being and usher in the entry of the capital punishment in the penal code as opposed to the alleged inadequacy of guidrigildo. Being the main Institutions, the Church with its Fathers and Popes, and the Roman law, could wield the necessary power to modify the previous situation. In order to support this point, it seems trivial—although necessary—to refer to the infamous Holy Inquisition, which came to light at the end of the twelfth century. However, there are many points Mereu makes on this issue, if I will mention just a few, and not all of them to detriment of the Inquisition. First, the Church justified the death penalty, in spite of the Gospels, through some rhetorical ruses that aimed at emphasizing the distinction between what Ideology must teach, and what, instead, must be effectively done (the motto of old that priests used to say was "do what I say, do not do what I do..."). The church aimed, basically, at putting in charge the secular power of the lethal function to restore the supposedly subverted order.[85] Second, the machine of the Inquisition began to work efficiently, (namely) the way (that) common knowledge recalls, only after the Council of Trent, in 1563. Third and more relevant to the purpose of my paper, is to describe the inquisitorial method to collect evidence of the alleged crime. To highlight the importance of the point, Mereu states:

> This is the moment in which begins and will become fully effective that deep juridical revolution in the field of penal and trial law that, through the legitimization of the suspect, and the creation of the inquisitorial system...will modify the whole European penal and trial law, whose effects are still lasting.[86]

The prevalence of the Medieval Inquisitorial system over the prior Roman Adversary proceeding heavily modifies the balance of power between the actors at the trial, by dint of the inversion of the burden of proof. The Inquisitor accuses you, with or without evidence, and you must prove your innocence. This meant that the Inquisitor could put you in prison in total absence of evidence, using the whole range of means and devices at his disposal in order to make you "confess." Nowadays, in Italy, they justify long detention before trial on the basis of the existence of *prove indiziarie*—a formula hard to translate, a sort of collection of clues that *might* point to illegal behavior. The adoption of this neological code most often, merely reveals a way to corrupt the language *and* to justify the inquisitorial method. It also gives an inkling of the violent and powerful character law still displays and deploys.

Mereu suggests that the principles informing the fearful law are few, but very successful in accomplishing their function: 1) "consenso o repressione" (consent or repression), which can be extrapolated from Saint Augustine's teachings; 2) "normativa rinnegante" (reneging norm) 3) "teoria organica" (organic or synecdochic theory, as I prefer to name it). The ground upon which they all rest is *utilitas,* sometimes also differently labeled as *necessitas.* It is worth noting that, having utility and necessity as polar stars, the legislator conceives the law according to principles awkwardly intertwined—if they are presented with concepts such as, justice and truth, as I will show later on. One of these principles is evoked by Jacques Derrida in quoting the seventeenth century French philosopher Blaise Pascal, where the latter reminds us that custom, *coutume,* has the power of authority: "Custom is the sole basis for equity, for the simple reason that it is received; it is the mystical foundation of its authority."[87] Despite Pascal's thought and Derrida's support, we nonetheless have to account for changes in custom, as I have mentioned at the beginning of my paper, for instance the one that takes place when we witness the switch from *guidrigildo* to the death penalty. Mereu's principles shed light precisely on the point of intersection between custom and change. In fact: "consent or repression" is a principle describing an enforcement of law through violence. Consent to my *new* idea, or I will repress you. New, in this case, is the idea of the State and its juridical-political dimension. (These are the centuries in which the concept of sovereignty will attract the interest of political thinkers, which they will borrow from law, since, "As for Middle Age, one can define State of Law in the sense that the State receives strength and authority from the Law and it is sustained and dominated by it...Sovereignty is not a political but a juridical concept, and represents the typical medieval idea that the *princeps* founds the Law because he occupies the sovereign position.")[88] In addition, as we have seen, new is also the Church's reaction against what it considered heresy. New is, consequently, the punishment. Walter Benjamin put forward a similar theory in his *Critique of Violence,* in which he explained his theory of the double character of violence, defined as lawmaking and law-preserving violence. For example, he maintained that the "death penalty in primitive legal systems is imposed even for such crimes as offenses against property [because] its purpose is not to punish the infringement of law but to establish new law. For in the exercise of violence over life and death, more than in any other legal act, the law reaffirms itself."[89] Not only does the law reaffirm itself through violence; Benjamin adds that "one might perhaps consider the possibility that the law's interest in a monopoly of violence vis-à-vis individuals is explained not by the intention of preserving legal ends but, rather, by the intention of preserving the law itself."[90] This provides us with a valuable insight about the very need of the existence of the capital penalty in the first place, regardless of the crimes it is bound to punish. Does this mean that Benjamin is in favor of the death penalty? Derrida's elaboration will help to clarify this point:

> The violence that conserves ("law-preserving violence"), this threat which is not intimidation, is a threat of *droit*. Double genitive: it both comes from and threatens *droit*...Benjamin seems to think that the arguments against the *droit de punir* and notably against the death penalty are superficial, and not by accident. For they do not admit an axiom essential to the definition of law. Which? Well, when one tackles the death penalty, one doesn't dispute one penalty among the others but law itself in its origin, in its very order. If the origin of law is a violent positioning, the latter manifests itself in the purest fashion when violence is absolute, that is to say when it touches the right to life and to death.[91]

Therefore, the question as to whether Benjamin was in favor of the death penalty is simply (an) erroneously posed (one). Given the inherent double character of law, the relationship between death penalty and law can be portrayed as a relationship between means (a pure one, Benjamin said) and an end, where the aim is the preservation of the latter by dint of the former. The conclusion one can reach, after these considerations, is extremely stunning, namely that to live in a State of Right (*État de Droit*) constantly puts one's life at stake, as though one is living in a topsy-turvy Hobbesean world where the Covenant shields you from external foe while threatening you at any given moment.

The analysis becomes more and more intriguing when we consider Mereu's "reneging norm," according to which the *general* law (for instance, the divine commandment "Thou shalt not kill") can be violated if the *specific* law, ruled by utility or necessity, as we know, grants it. The effectiveness of the reneging of the norm depends on how profoundly the "organic theory" has become part of the collective imaginary, and this closes the vicious circle. In Benjamin's words, the commandment exists in order to prevent the deed, but "the injunction becomes inapplicable, incommensurable, once the deed is accomplished...[The commandment] exists not as a criterion of judgment, but as a guideline for the actions of persons or communities who have to wrestle with it in solitude and, in exceptional cases, to take on themselves the responsibility of ignoring it."[92] This deliberate ignorance of the commandment can be considered as the prelude to the violent reaffirmation of law mentioned earlier, an act that finally Benjamin calls "divine violence, which is the sign and seal but never the means of sacred dispatch, [and it] may be called "sovereign" violence."[93] The ambiguous, "divine" and at the same time violent and constituting power of law (somewhat beyond good and evil, one may say) is once again rephrased by Derrida. Says the French scholar:

> The very emergence of justice and law implies a performative force, which is always an interpretative force[94]...in the sense of law that would maintain a more internal, more complex relation with what one calls force, power or violence...Its

> very moment of foundation or institution..., the operation that amounts to founding, inaugurating, justifying law (*droit*), making law, would consist of a *coup de force,* of a performative and therefore interpretative violence that in itself is neither just nor unjust and that no justice and no previous law with its founding anterior moment could guarantee or contradict or invalidate.[95]

Derrida's quotation lingers around two very important points that imply and determine each other, one we have already met and a second one merely evoked but has remained unexplored thus far: the inherent violence of law and the belief. To begin with, what sort of *croyance,* belief, is evoked by Derrida? A mystic belief, he says. At any rate, it is not just a question involving religious topics, an issue that remains inside the legitimate spiritual sphere. Once again, we are dealing with a borderline concept, better said, a *bridging* one, since it creates a connection—if undefined and, we will see in short, describable only through negations—between two originally heterogeneous realms. Because "The precise details of an emergency cannot be anticipated, nor can one spell out what may take place in such a case... from the liberal constitutional point of view, there would be no competence at all."[96] The lack of "competence," so to say, is an aspect that Benjamin underscores as well, when he states that one cannot rule out the death penalty relying on the divine commandment:

> No judgment of the deed can be derived from the commandment. And so neither the divine judgment nor the grounds for this judgment can be known in advance. Those who base a condemnation of all violent killing of one person by another on the commandment are therefore mistaken.[97]

Divine commandments work as guidelines, as we saw above, but they do not prevent infringements that need to be restored, afterward, mostly through violent acts. Therefore, one may say that Schmitt, Benjamin, and Derrida agree on the fact that law finds its foundation outside the legal field, above all in violence. It is precisely at this point that mystical proves necessary to strengthen law with *authority* so that the latter makes the former heard and abode by. Authority is all law needs to achieve its goals, given that "*autoritas [sic], non veritas facit legem*"[98] [authority makes law, not truth] but it also holds true the other way around, since "*Auctoritas* is not sufficient in itself; whether it authorizes or ratifies, it implies an extraneous activity that it validates."[99] Hence, in order to be effective, law and authority need to shore each other up, and yet the mechanism seems to perfectly work only if their heterogeneity is mystified and thereby made acceptable to those who are ruled by them. The "mystic halo" (and, again, a sort of lack of competence) of law is emphasized by Derrida, when he quotes what Michel de Montaigne—and Pascal after him—said about law, namely that "laws were not in themselves just but rather were just only because they were laws."[100] In other words, this mystic halo covers up and implements both law and authority, enforcing the legal system in a violent way while it obnubilates its elusive double structure. In so far as this earthly power represents the state body, it also, and at the same time, according to medieval political thought, stands for the celestial *corpus mysticum,* so that the latter, higher, order has to be reflected in the former, lower. The sinners, who are the infected part, need to be punished as well and sent to Hell or Purgatory so that they cannot corrupt the whole mystical body, correspondingly the criminals need to be severed from the healthy body of the state. The synecdochic theory, in fact, the third of Mereu's principles, works precisely when it supposedly preserves the State through the elimination of its alleged rotten parts. According to the principle, then, the State, not only can, but must destroy its elected enemy in order to prosper and improve. One can claim, hence, that when sovereignty installs as the mystic foundation of the political entity (through a rhetoric of utility and necessity that in its final and accomplished stage becomes *law*), the road to any form of "state of emergency," or "exception," with all that comes along with it including all its consequences, has just been paved. It is precisely when rhetoric and sovereignty meet, having as a goal to fuel and protect each other, that we come across the most effective—and dreadfully lethal—products of politics.

Plato, writing his *Republic,* mainly aimed at providing his audience with an uplifting sample of engaged literature, as the critic would have said in the 70's. Certainly, he did not conceive of himself as the legislator of Athens, and violence played no role in his game. In other words, the idea of a sovereignty to be protected and defended against some endemic or foreign enemy was *not* his main concern. He wrote as an educator, perhaps just making up the *Socratic* midwife that fills all his pages. But when you read an article of law (the Article 48 of the Weimar Constitution) stating that,

> If security and public order are seriously [*erheblich*] disturbed or threatened in the German Reich, the president of the Reich may take the measures necessary to reestablish security and public order, with the help of the armed forces if required. To this end he may wholly or partially suspend the fundamental rights [*Grundrechte*] established in Articles 114, 115, 117, 118, 123, 124, and 153,[101]

then you suddenly realize the inherent ambiguity of rhetoric in its foremost function of means towards an end. The discrepancy lies between rhetoric as a means to embody an educative factor (as in Plato), and rhetoric as a means to achieve political ends. Here, once again, we face the mystic and performative power of the discourse, as Derrida defines it: "the mystical. Here a silence is walled up in the violent structure of the founding act."[102] The founding act just mentioned, is the sanction—in its two contradictory meanings, namely encouragement and coercive measure—of the "state of exception," the juridical entity that founds, as Agamben reminds us, on a void ("What the 'ark' of power contains at its center is the state of exception—but this is essentially an empty space, in which a human action with no relation to law stands before a norm with no relation to life"[103]) created through the very means of the rhetoric of fear, a discourse that claims to defend us against an ineffable and often surreptitious peril while it takes away our fundamental civil rights; one might define it the cunning of rhetoric, as in the Article 48 mentioned earlier. Carl Schmitt, in his *Political Theology,* is crystal clear about the exception at issue: "What characterizes an exception is principally unlimited authority, which means the suspension of the entire existing order."[104] We are again dealing with the power of life and death over the citizens, in the upside down Hobbesean realm. From the platonic "ruler" of a symmetric and balanced political body to the violent "suspender" of the existing order via the death penalty, we have thus covered the entire distance between Chaos and Cosmos: backward, unfortunately. Schmitt, Benjamin, Derrida, and Agamben among others, have been describing this trajectory to our benefit. They have been providing us with words and theories to better grasp the phenomenon concerning the precariousness of our status as citizens. However, I set out my essay with Italo Mereu and his detailed history of *La morte come pena* because I was trying to make the point that law determines exceptions each and every time it exerts what the Roman Law, as Foucault and Agamben remind us, named *vitae necisque potestas,* the power of life and death. As Benjamin said in his eighth Thesis *On the Concept of History,* "The tradition of the oppressed teaches us that the 'state of emergency' in which we live is not the exception but the rule." It is a lethal, and by definition fascist rule, because a) all the rights are suspended, and b) it tends to become an institution, rather than a sporadic resource, which keeps harping on the "river of biopolitics that gave *homo sacer* his life [and] runs its course in a hidden but continuous fashion."[105] Accordingly, we, all of us, are constantly at the mercy of the sovereign power, whatever shape it possesses. Carlo Cattaneo wrote that "from a ferocious political reaction nobody, *nobody,* is safe. The guillotine spared neither friends nor foes; it spared neither servants nor kings."[106] That is why the death penalty, in my view, is simply one among manifold signs that our society has still to rise from the Kantian "state of minority" in which it has been immersed thus far. The legal violence nourishes on rhetoric *and* fear; perhaps, the task we are left with nowadays is to tie the knot between what rhetoric evokes and fear accomplishes, by dint of a different political relationship between human beings and institutions.

PART II

STATE OF EXCEPTION:

FROM HISTORY TO LITERATURE

CHAPTER FIVE

MAX HENNINGER

PATCHWORK, 1979: NOTES ON *BLACKOUT* BY NANNI BALESTRINI

Blackout, an extended poem by Nanni Balestrini published in 1980, offers an unusually suggestive account of the prolonged "state of exception" the Italian republic found itself in for more than a decade following the labor militancy and social protest of the late 1960s. The poem was written in 1979, the year of the massive legal repression that saw its author being charged, like numerous other political activists and intellectuals, with collusion in the activities of the Red Brigades (the clandestine organization that kidnapped and murdered Aldo Moro, the president of the Italy's Christian Democrat Party, in 1978). Balestrini escaped to France before he could be arrested, remaining there until after all charges were dropped (for lack of evidence) in June 1984. When *Blackout* was published in Italy by the Feltrinelli publishing house, its author was therefore the object of that particularly aggressive brand of persecution made possible by the various special laws passed in Italy during the 1970s, a persecution whose effects continue to haunt the country today.

In *Blackout*, the year of Balestrini's escape becomes a vantage point from which the turbulent history of the Italian 1970s can be recounted. Balestrini's reflections on 1979 address the major cultural, economic, and political transformations of the time. No doubt the sheer scope of Balestrini's themes constitutes one of the reasons why the poem has long been neglected by critics. Besides being characterized by an unusual degree of intertextuality, *Blackout* requires a more accurate knowledge of its historical and biographical context than is the case with Balestrini's earlier and later publications.

The pages that follow present an overview of some of the most significant events of the period narrated by Balestrini. This overview will serve as the basis for a reading of *Blackout* that explores some of the thematic and historical links between this work and a variety of theoretical models from the fields of politics, economics, and philosophy—models ranging from the innovative conception of class struggle developed within the Italian Marxism of the 1960s and 1970s to the theory of space formulated by French poststructuralists Gilles Deleuze and Félix Guattari. By relating *Blackout* to some of the more influential intellectual currents associated with 1979, it will become possible to situate the poem within the complex cultural and socio-political circumstances from which it emerged, circumstances to which it continuously directs the reader's attention.

It will be best to begin surveying the period narrated in *Blackout* by considering *operaismo,* the current of Marxism that emerged in Italy with the appearance of the journals *Quaderni rossi* and *Classe operaia* during the early 1960s.[107] *Operaismo* constituted an attempt to formulate a conceptual apparatus and a practical strategy that would do justice to the transformation of the Italian working class during the period of postwar reconstruction; it also sought to take account of the problematic character of Soviet Marxism as highlighted by the outcome of the Hungarian insurrection of 1956. The distinctive trait of *operaismo* consisted in its insistence on the autonomy and primacy of working-class struggle with regard to capitalist planning. For the theorists of *operaismo,* the working class needed to be thought of not as passively responding to the transformations of capitalism as imposed by entrepreneurs, but rather as the driving force behind those transformations. As one of the leading theorists of *operaismo,* Mario Tronti, wrote in "Lenin in Inghilterra," a 1964 essay that was to become the centrepiece of his classic *Operai e capitale* (1966):

> We too have seen capitalist development as preceding labor struggles. It's a mistake. The problem needs to be turned on its head, examined in a different light, by returning to the starting point, and the starting point is the working class. Once capital has developed on a social scale, capitalist development is subordinated to labor struggles; it follows them and must make the political mechanism of its production process correspond to them.[108]

During the 1960s, Tronti and other early exponents of *operaismo* layed the groundwork for what would soon be called "autonomist Marxism." Against programs of collective bargaining that aimed at the progressive integration of communist organizations into the politico-economic structures of the Italian republic (such as the Italian Communist Party's policy of *programmazione democratica*), the *operaisti* insisted on the radical antagonism between labor and capital. They argued that this antagonism could only become more pronounced as the large-scale introduction of Fordist production techniques accelerated capitalism's dependence on masses of highly mobile and de-skilled labor (the *operaio massa* or "mass worker"). The new Italian working class was both more fully subsumed under capitalist command than the earlier class of skilled workers (the *operaio professionale* or "craft worker") and more likely to radically contest that command—more than ever, labor was "within capital and opposed to it," in Tronti's famous phrase.[109] In this sense, Italy's "economic miracle" provided a unique opportunity for a working class-insurrection: "Capitalist society's economic take-off provides the historical opportunity for a socialist revolution."[110] The new revolutionary project would be premised on a working-class strategy of radical non-collaboration—an uncompromising rejection not only of collective bargaining, but of wage labor itself (the *strategia del rifiuto* or "strategy of refusal"):

> Abstaining from work means rejecting the command exercised by capital as the organizer of production. It means saying 'no' to the proposition of concrete work at a specific point. It's a *momentaneous* stalling of the work process as the recurring threat that empties the valorization process of its content.[111]

This was more than a theory. Wildcat strikes became increasingly common in Italy from the mid-1960s onward, as did violent clashes between labor and the police. In 1966, Siemens workers in Milan formed a strike committee in complete independence from the trade unions. The same year, trade union membership reached a historical low in Italy. (Membership in the Italian Communist Party also declined dramatically in strategic locations such as FIAT's Mirafiori factory.) 1966 was a year of major contract negotiations—that is, one in which one would expect a large number of strikes. In fact, the number of hours spent on strike continued to increase after 1966, and Angelo Costa, the president of the Italian industrial league *Confindustria*, would soon be heard to exclaim: "Make sure Italians don't lose their desire to work."[112]

Labor's progressive alienation from the bargaining strategies of the Communist Party and the trade unions was evidenced, in 1968, by the formation of *Comitati unitari di base* [Unified Shopfloor Committees] (CUBs). The CUBs formed throughout Italy, from Milan to Naples and Porto Torres, Sardinia. As rank-and-file organizations that brought together workers from different trade unions, the CUBs effectively undermined the strategy of "divide and conquer" that had made possible the system of *gabbie salariali* (that is, the system of "wage cages" that entailed paying different wages for the same work in different regions of Italy). They constituted an important symptom of the process of radical re-composition the Italian working class was undergoing at the time, in addition to confirming *operaismo*'s claims about labor's growing unity and autonomy.

Working-class militancy reached a first climax during the *Autunno caldo* [Hot Autumn] of 1969, which saw close to 40,000 FIAT workers on strike in Turin.[113] By October 1969, general strikes and demonstrations were being held across the country. They were indicative of an important shift from economic to political contestation. On November 19th, workers in Turin organized a national strike for housing. Across the country, a highly politicized working class resisted increases in rent, electricity, and transportation fares by what would later be called the strategy of *autoriduzione,* forcing concessions from the major service corporations by a generalized abstention from payment.[114]

In Italy, 1969 constituted an extension of the exceptional socio-political situation associated in other countries with 1968. The labor struggles of 1969 were linked to the student unrest of previous years.[115] Throughout 1968 and 1969, students declared their solidarity with labor. The *consigli di deputati* organized by workers in a number of Italian factories included many student members. The common front formed by students and labor was also evident in the formation of various extra-parliamentary groups, such as *Lotta continua* and *Potere operaio,* during the period 1968-69.[116]

These groups would continue their activities until the mid-1970s, when many of them dissolved in order to give way to the much more diffuse network of social protest movements commonly known as the *movimento del '77,* sometimes simply called *il Movimento.*[117] Among the early symptoms of the Movement's emergence was the creation of the first *centri sociali* in the suburbs of Milan and other cities. The social centres were squatted buildings converted into communal spaces for political discussion and cultural activities (such as concerts, theatrical performances, and the production of underground journals). A number of them still exist today. They were set up not so much by workers and students as by the unemployed or underemployed youth populating the suburbs of northern Italy.[118] Many members of the Movement were unemployed university graduates, often with a proletarian background. (In Italy as elsewhere, there had been a massive influx of workers into the university system during the 1960s.)

Despite its name, the Movement of 1977 was involved in clashes with the police as early as 1976, the year it set out to block access to Milan's opera house, *La Scala,* drawing some 5000 policemen and *carabinieri* and bringing about a night of streetfights that left a toll of several dozen injured protesters. In 1977, the year that Education Minister Malfatti attempted to roll back many of the concessions won by students in 1968, the Movement organized a new wave of university occupations and demonstrations. Several policemen and protesters were killed during the street clashes that erupted throughout Italy in March 1977—clashes that saw the raising of barricades and the devastation of downtown areas in several cities, and which prompted the police and the *carabinieri* to implement military tactics (such as the use of tanks during the battle for Bologna University on March 13th).

Despite these episodes of violence, which the government responded to with emergency laws and by repeatedly suspending the constitutional right to demonstrate, the Movement was to a significant extent a cultural phenomenon. Its music and theatre festivals (such as that held in Bologna in September 1977) brought together tens of thousands of young Italians. The Movement created new spaces for cultural and social activity (such as the *centri sociali)* and new channels for creative expression (in the form, for example, of its oppositional radio stations, the *radio libere*). Premised on a generalized rejection of Fordist factory labor, it reflected not just the *socializzazione della lotta* [socialization of the struggle] that striking FIAT workers had called for in 1969, but also the culmination of a lengthy process of proletarian *autovalorizzazione.* That is, it successfully created a host of new and autonomous social spaces, setting out not only to reject the logic of the market, but also to find alternatives to that logic.[119] It in this sense that Franco Berardi (Bifo) has argued that "the Movement of '77 represents, in all its aspects—social, political, and cultural—the moment of culmination of the class struggle in Italy."[120]

The Movement was, however, short-lived. By 1980, most of its members were in prison. Many of its journals had ceased publication, and its radio stations had been shut down. To some extent, the defeat of the Movement was made possible by an escalation in the series of kidnappings and assassinations carried out by clandestine left-wing organizations such as the Red Brigades. (The 1978 kidnapping and murder of Aldo Moro, president of the Italian Christian Democrat Party, constituted the bloody and traumatic climax of Red Brigades activities in Italy.) While never more than a fringe group (its membership is not thought ever to have exceeded 200), the Red Brigades succeeded, by their spectacular operations, in becoming the focus of public attention. They had formed, like a host of smaller insurrectionary groups, in the period after December of 1969, when a neo-fascist terrorist operation—the planting of a bomb in Milan's National Agricultural Bank, which killed 16 civilians and injured 87—had led to a massive crackdown not so much on neo-fascist as on left-wing groups.[121] It was in the wake of this crackdown that a number of left-wing organizations had opted for clandestinity; some had developed a program of *lotta armata* and begun carrying out kidnappings and assassinations.[122]

By the late 1970s, the heavy toll of terrorist violence—carried out by groups of both left-wing and right-wing persuasion, but associated in the public mind mainly with the left—made possible a major campaign of criminal persecution of which the Movement and the *operaisti* were the main victims. The mass arrests of April 7, 1979 were justified by reference to the so-called *teorema Calogero,* named after the public prosecutor who ordered the arrests. The *teorema Calogero* postulated the existence of a single left-wing insurrectionary group, comprising both a clandestine "military" section (the Red Brigades) and a network of non-clandestine members (the activists of the Movement, and those of the most prominent extra-parliamentary formation of those years, *Autonomia operaia*). Calogero was able to accuse left-wing activists associated with the Movement of being directly linked to terrorist operations such as the

Moro kidnapping. Many members of the Movement were incarcerated in newly constructed *prigioni speciali* [high-security prisons] along with convicted terrorists. A significant number of the arrests were made in the absence of material evidence (that is, purely on the basis of written or oral statements). By 1980, Italy was second only to the Soviet Union for its number of political prisoners (more than 15,000). A number of the accused were held for several years before the charges were dropped for lack of evidence; some 200 remain in prison today, and roughly the same number have been living in exile for the past two decades in order to avoid arrest.[123]

As noted, Nanni Balestrini was himself one of the activists for whom arrest warrants were issued on April 7th. An acclaimed writer who had become politicized in 1968, and who had participated in the creation of the extra-parliamentary group *Potere operaio* in 1969, Balestrini was accused by Calogero of various crimes ranging from inciting insurrectionary violence to complicity in Red Brigades terrorism. Balestrini's escape to France marked the beginning of several years of exile; he has since returned to Italy.

The 48-page poem *Blackout* was Balestrini's first book-length publication following his escape from Italy. It was originally intended as the libretto for a vocal performance by Demetrio Stratos, the singer of Area, a progressive rock group closely associated with the Movement of 1977. Balestrini meant to base his libretto on newspaper reports of the riots that occured following the 1979 electricity blackout in New York. When Stratos unexpectedly died of leukemia shortly afterwards, Balestrini began to re-conceptualize his writing project. In its final version, *Blackout* reflects not just on the death of Stratos, but also on Balestrini's legal persecution and the decline of the Movement more generally. As Gian Paolo Renello has written, the poem presents itself largely as an extended meditation on the themes of death and defeat:

> The death of Demetrio Stratos; the end of an era, that of '68; the destruction of the individual by the oppressive and harmful rite of factory labor; the judicial rite, experienced as a form of persecution; the collective rite of the blackout, where violence of all kinds is unleashed in a destructive process that presents itself as an example of liberty—these are some of the metaphors of death that recur insistently and obsessively in the text. Death as an inevitable process and the end of a cycle.[124]

Blackout is indeed one of Balestrini's most sombre texts, far removed, for example, from the triumphalism of his 1971 novel *Vogliamo tutto*, which chronicles the emergence of the new political subject that was the *operaio massa*. The revolutionary project of *operaismo* is presented in *Blackout* as a stalled process, and much of the poem deals with the themes of repression and persecution. Only the passages devoted to the New York riots of 1979 suggest that the revolutionary project of *operaismo* may be alive and well; the riots function as a synecdoche of the cycle of labor struggles that shook Italy for more than a decade following the events of 1968. Yet *Blackout* closes not so much with a vision of successful anti-capitalist contestation as with images of helplessness, futility, and desolation.

Properly understanding *Blackout* requires some knowledge of Balestrini's idiosyncratic techniques of literary composition. Ever since his emergence on the Italian literary scene as one of the most prominent members of the Italian *neoavanguardia,* Balestrini has championed a radically non-linear and anti-subjectivist form of writing. Both in his poetry and in his novels, Balestrini has consistently refused to write what would ordinarily be thought of as original texts. His works are montages of passages culled from a wide-range of pre-existing documents: interviews, television and radio broadcasts, newspaper articles, novels, political pamphlets, and trial transcripts. (*Blackout* also includes photographs.) Angelo Guglielmi has even been able to define Balestrini's method of literary composition purely in terms of the calculated assemblage of passages selected from pre-existing documents. The assemblage is a calcuated one in that it is performed in accordance with a strict formal scheme. Balestrini's writing becomes, for Guglielmi, not so much the spontaneous self-expression of a single narrator as a quasi-mathematical process of "organization of signs."[125]

Perhaps the most extreme example of this method of composition is offered by Balestrini's 1961 poem "Tape Mark 1," which was assembled, with the aid of an IBM computer, from phrases taken from the *Tao Te King* and two works of literature (*Hiroshima Diary* by Michihito Hachiya and *Mystery of the Elevator* by Paul Goldwin). *À propos* of this poem, Edoardo Sanguineti has spoken of "una poesia *ex machina*" and of

> A calculated combination that explicitly presents itself as one selection from the endless number of combinations allowed for by the underlying linguistic material, in a universe formed entirely of mere possibilities and linguistic combinations.[126]

By his use of montage, Balestrini creates texts that do not so much unfold linear narratives as assemble disjunct semantic elements, between which the reader is invited to make his own connections. Balestrini's combinatory procedure becomes, as it were, a call to the reader to engage in a process of creative re-combination. Renato Barilli has suggested that, in this sense, Balestrini breaks with the traditional temporal paradigm of narrative writing, creating a literature that is more properly spatial:

> The various fragments can spread across several pages or superimpose themselves upon one another on a single page, intersecting each other, connecting according to the logic of the chessboard, transversally, horizontally, and vertically, as in a crossword puzzle.[127]

All of these characteristics of Balestrini's technique of composition are starkly evident in *Blackout.* The poem consists exclusively of pre-existing documents. They include newspaper articles on the 1979 New York blackout, Calogero's arrest warrant for Balestrini, and a personal letter.[128] These documents are assembled in accordance with a geometrical scheme reproduced in the appendix to the poem. The scheme is based on the pattern of a patchwork quilt, a photograph of which is inserted between the poem's dedication—"*Per i compagni perseguitati/ 7 aprile 1980*" [For the persecuted comrades / 7 April 1980]—and its opening section. The scheme of composition calls for an arrangement of the poem's various sources that allows for vertical, horizontal, and diagonal combinations. A brief description of this scheme is indispensable for understanding the poem.

The scheme takes the form of a square sub-divided into four vertically arranged rectangles (one rectangle is placed above the other). Each rectangle corresponds to one of the poem's four sections and is divided into 12 vertical columns, corresponding to the 12 pages of each section. If Balestrini had left the scheme like this, his poem would certainly have been neatly organized, but it would have retained the linear character his compositions almost invariably set out to subvert. In order to introduce the possibility of what Barilli calls a "transversal reading," Balestrini's scheme reproduces not just the vertical and horizontal or grid-like structure of the quilt, but also a diagonal division.[129] Each of the four rectangles is traversed by four diagonal lines. In this way, each rectangle is subdivided into three parallelograms and (at its outer edges) two triangles. The entire scheme is thereby made up of a total of 20 spaces (five spaces—that is, three parallelograms and two triangles—within each of the four rectangles). Each of these 20 spaces corresponds to one of the documents used by Balestrini.

Because the columns corresponding to the pages of each section are vertical, they cut across the diagonal lines; that is, they cut from one space (triangle or parallelogram) into another. This means that on every page of the poem, there is a shift—unannounced, if the reader does not check the scheme—from one document to another. The poem does progress gradually from the first document to the last, but this progression does not occur in step with the division of each section into 12 pages: the order of the pages is based on a vertical division of the scheme, that of the sources on a diagonal division.

To appreciate the effect of such a structure, one need only read the first page of *Blackout.* Save for its last line, the first page assembles phrases taken exclusively from the first of Balestrini's sources (a description of Mont Blanc taken from a tourist map). Just as the reader has grown accustomed to the extended description of a sublime mountain landscape—"grandiose panorama on the giant glacier and the glistening mountains that rise above it…crisp colours profiles scattered clouds heavy with rain dashes of azure"—he is jolted out of his reverie by the phrase "an azure stream of jeans."[130] What has happened? Balestrini has simply obeyed his scheme of composition and shifted to his second document, a newspaper report on the memorial concert held for Stratos in June 1979.[131] The beginning of the next page will switch back briefly to the description of Mont Blanc, only to return after a few lines to the news report. And so the poem continues.[132]

While he never strays from his scheme of composition, Balestrini has obviously thought carefully about his selection of documents and their distribution on the scheme. In the passage just quoted, this emerges clearly from the association between "dashes of azure" and "an azure stream of jeans." As Guglielmi already pointed out in discussing Balestrini's early work, this kind of technique of composition

> Only appears to be mechanical, since...it presupposes a number of interventions and delicate decisions, each of which has significant consequences.[133]

The elegance of the composition—"an icy elegance" in Guglielmi's apt phrase—results precisely from this combination of strict formal principles and careful attention to linguistic and semantic nuances.[134] It is worth adding that, by including images in his set of documents, the Balestrini of *Blackout* also displays an acute awareness of the visual aspects of composition. Much as the textual documents appear at greater or lesser length on various pages, the images appear sometimes in full and sometimes only in part, but always in such a way as to resonate powerfully with the text. For example, the final page of *Blackout*'s first section is almost entirely taken up by a daunting aerial photograph of Manhattan, above which appear only a few lines of text:

> There's no hope in the factory
> in the city disaggregrated by immigration rendered inhuman
> by the ghetto neighborhoods where the quality of life is dramatic.[135]

The titles of the four sections of *Blackout*—"Trasformazione," "Istigazione," "Persecuzione," and "Inibizione"—are all accompanied by a different English-language definition of the word "blackout." The first definition—"a loss of memory of an event or fact"—identifies some of the major themes of the first section: loss, discontinuity, forgetting.[136] The remaining three definitions accord similarly with the themes of the sections they precede. The second section, which features passages from newspaper reports on the riots during the 1979 electricity blackout in New York, is preceded by the definition "the extinguishing of all stage lights to end a play or scene."[137] The third section, devoted to the events of April 1979 in Italy and featuring excerpts from media reports on those events, as well as from Calogero's arrest warrant for Balestrini, opens with the definition "suppression censorship concealment etc."[138] The fourth section, which turns centrally on the description of a nervous crisis as suffered during solitary confinement, is allotted the definition "a momentary lapse of consciousness or vision."[139]

It is worth considering each of these sections more closely. The first—which consists largely of a description of the memorial concert for Stratos—is devoted to the memory of the concerts and festivals organized by the Movement, and, more generally, to the memory of the spirit of 1968. This vibrant spirit of protest is presented as something that has been lost, although it also continues to haunt the present—like a memory one can neither fully evoke nor suppress. Besides this sense of a temporal remove (between 1968 and the present), there is also one of spatial separation: the mountain landscape described on the opening pages evokes the route by which Balestrini escaped from Italy into France.

As suggested earlier, the New York riots that are the focus of the second section function as a synecdoche for the political unrest that shook Italy during the 1960s and 1970s.[140] Balestrini focuses particularly on the looting that occurred during the riots. The phrase "we mean to take what we want and we want what we need" evokes the slogan from 1969 that Balestrini used as the title for his first political novel, *Vogliamo tutto.*[141] Phrases such as "prices have risen too much there'll be no more prices now Broadway will be gone when we're through" and "a 50-year-old woman walks into the store with a shopping bag saying today we shop for free" recall the practices of *autoriduzione* and *espropriazione,* as well as the popular slogan "Prices keep going up / Let's take what we need and stop paying."[142] The phrase "a woman called me on the phone and said they're stampeding down Bushwick Avenue like a herd of buffaloes" recalls the media reports concerning the arrival of an *orda vandalica* that circulated prior to the Movement's 1976 blockade of *La Scala.*[143] An article on the imminent crash landing of the US space station Skylab, cited towards the end of the section, suggests impending doom for one of US capitalism's most extravagantly financed projects, and perhaps even for US capitalism itself. In the chapter of *Vogliamo tutto* titled "L'Assemblea," Balestrini had already portrayed the aerospace industry as a prime example of capitalism's crass squandering of resources.[144]

The third section of *Blackout*, devoted to the theme of state repression, begins by evoking once more Balestrini's escape from France. The document with which the section opens is a passage from Ugo Foscolo's *Ultime Lettere di Jacopo Ortis,* describing the narrator's imminent escape from Italy: "Send your letters to Nice because tomorrow I'm leaving for France and perhaps for somewhere more distant."[145] Another suggestive phrase from Foscolo—"persecute your persecutors with the truth"—precedes extended quotations from the arrest warrant issued by "dr. pietro calogero the state prosecutor."[146] The section also juxtaposes some of the more slanderous media reports on those arrested in April 1979—"victims of the frustration left by that senseless '68 refugees of an impatient and immodest politics blindly racing down the path called 'never again without a gun'"—with the description of a zombie taken from a book on vampires: "It's a corpse reduced to a mute automaton that docilely follows every order."[147] This juxtaposition allows for at least two interpretations: that Italy's journalists have been reduced to zombies controlled by the state, or that the state's crackdown on the Movement is motivated by a desire to replace the country's vibrant protest culture with a generalized state of mindless obedience.[148]

Blackout's closing section is by far the most complex. It offers the starkest images of state repression, including a description of a nervous breakdown in prison and a photograph of the crushed brain of protester Giovanni Zibbecchi, who was run over by a police van at a demonstration in Milan on April 17, 1975. The description of the nervous breakdown—based on a first-person account penned by German autonomist Karl Heinz Roth—is evocative of a more general condition of powerlessness and disintegration, thereby recalling the decline of the Movement following the arrests of 1979. Indeed, Balestrini urges the reader to make this connection by placing the phrase "inside forty fifty million people" directly after the description of a prison.[149] The suggestion is of course that 40,000 or 50,000 people have been incarcerated. In fact, the phrase is taken from a report on the concert that was the focus of *Blackout*'s opening section. (Balestrini has arranged his sources in such a way that a number of motifs from earlier in the poem recur towards the end.) Even after one has realized this, however, the effect remains a powerful one. The evocation of "forty fifty thousand people," followed soon after by a reference to "the sense of finding myself in an Italian conundrum which for years has remained unresolved unchanged" assumes a tragic note in the context of the closing section's general evocation of repression and helplessness.[150]

As if to emphasize the sordid character of the Movement's defeat, Balestrini does not allow this tragic note to persist. Instead, he shifts to the description of a banal holiday outing. The outing involves a stalled engine and a disappointing arrival at a decrepit house infested with "insects of every kind bird nests in the windows dead birds pheasants darting about everywhere." These images of desolation and disappointment are linked to a sense of lethargy, "a constant tiredness a state of generalized torpor accompanied by yawns." They are also related to a condition of fear, "a common fear of being alone."[151] All this offers a depressing contrast to the images of youthful revolt and the sense of the sublime that feature in earlier sections of the poem.

Yet woven into this evocation of a state of paralysis and fear—the state of "inhibition" that the section's title announces—are repeated references to an approaching "great storm" and to "overwhelming rage"—each of these phrases recurs three times.[152] The reader is led to expect a dramatic event, and the section does indeed close with such an event—albeit one already familiar: namely, the electricity blackout that featured prominently in the second section. This time, Balestrini does not devote himself to the explosion of violence and crime that occurred during the blackout (phenomena that have positive connotations for him, as suggested above). Rather, he takes from the media reports on the blackout further images of disintegration and decline: "in the spent refrigerators frozen food begins to rot."[153] Some of the images evoked by Balestrini suggest disintegration on a grander and more threatening scale; this is the case, for example, with the image of Wall Street's "giant computers" shutting down.[154] Yet such passages do not so much suggest the violent destruction of capitalism as evoke its gradual implosion—an implosion that sits well with the other, more banal images of entropy and disintegration that feature in this section.

The closing words of the poem—"there was a collective guttural cry when the lights went out"—recall the images of crowds that feature in the first and second sections, yet the crowd is now no longer a joyful or subversive one (such as that at the Movement's concerts or the mob of rioters in New York). It evokes a generalized state of terror, linked to feelings of disorientation and helplessness: "hundreds of thousands of people try to get home or find shelter for the night."

There is one image on the closing page of *Blackout* that suggests hope, although it is also charged with irony: "only the torch of the Statue of Liberty remains lit thanks to a separate electricity source."[155] The allusion to the concept of *autonomia operaia* is obvious. Perhaps this image is best understood by reference to the closing image of *Gli invisibili,* a novel Balestrini published seven years after *Blackout*. *Gli invisibili* is devoted to the Movement of 1977 and the repression it suffered at the hands of the Italian state; it is as much a novel about prison violence and repression as about youthful revolt. The novel ends with a group of imprisoned members of the Movement holding torches out of the windows of their prison cells. The image suggests both defiance and futility:

> It must have been a beautiful spectacle from outside all of those trembling fires on the black prison wall in the middle of that endless plain but the only ones who

> could see the torches where those few car drivers that darted small and distant down the black highway several kilometres from the prison or maybe an airplane flying high above but they fly so high in the black and silent sky they don't see a thing.[156]

The bitterness of this passage is clearly akin to that of *Blackout*'s closing section. Yet there is more than just bitterness; there is also a sense that the state's victory over the Movement has not been total in that the protagonist has not been "reduced to a mute automaton that docilely follows every order."[157] The spirit of revolt has remained alive, even if it has been deprived of the conditions for action. In this sense, the recurrence of the blackout motif on the final pages of Balestrini's poem is ambiguous. The motif does recur in a general context of hopelessness; there remains a sense, however, that the spirit of 1968 will continue to haunt the present—"because it marked the beginning of an era and will continue to return."[158]

It seems appropriate to close with some reflections on the motif implicit throughout *Blackout*—that of the patchwork quilt. This is perhaps the most suggestive motif in the entire poem. It deserves to be analyzed by reference to its invocation both in the economic theory of autonomist Christian Marazzi and in the poststructuralist philosophy of Gilles Deleuze and Félix Guattari—a philosophy of which Antonio Negri and Michael Hardt have said that it constitutes the theoretical corollary to the struggles that occurred in Italy between 1968 and 1979.[159]

Balestrini's use of the motif extends beyond the photograph of the patchwork quilt that opens *Blackout.* In the first section of *Blackout,* the crowd at the 1979 rock concert is described as "a carpet that covers the seating rows and descends to spread over the entire field" and "a carpet of shoulders heads and arms that seems to move wavelike under gusts of wind." Between these two phrases, Balestrini inserts the words "one a thousand a hundred thousand voices for communicating."[160] The motif of the patchwork quilt is associated by Balestrini with a crowd—not the terrorized, disaggregated, and paralyzed crowd of the poem's closing section, but one characterized by constant motion and unfettered communication. As suggested above, this crowd is evocative of the wave of anti-capitalist struggles that was the Movement of 1977. It is both an example of proletarian autonomy as it resulted from the mass refusal of Fordist factory labor—"FIAT fears their hatred of the factory"—and an example of how such refusal can assume, as genuine *autovalorizzazione,* a joyful character: "the FIAT bosses have never seen the workers laugh and it makes them mad as hell."[161]

This reference to FIAT is worth emphasizing. Ever since the publication of *Vogliamo tutto* in 1971, FIAT has served in Balestrini's work as the prime example of a rigidly structured, functionally segmented capitalist space. From

Vogliamo tutto to *Gli invisibili,* Balestrini has portrayed revolutionary processes as processes of collective exit or flight—processes of *rifiuto* by which an emergent political subject vacates and dissolves the functional spaces to which it has been consigned.[162] This theme of new, nomadic subjects contesting the disciplinary spaces of Fordist capitalism is very much present in *Blackout,* where the nomadic subject is precisely the Movement of 1977, that patchwork of communicating individuals that vacate Italian society's most hierarchically organized institutions—the factory, the school, the university—and set out to create new, autonomous social and political spaces for themselves. The opening section of *Blackout* repeatedly contrasts the emergence of this new and unpredictable socio-political subject—"the public has presented itself in a different form and it has become something different"—with attempts to govern its rebellious lines of flight by re-imposing on them the functional and repetitive logic of Fordist production.[163] The latter is evoked by the recurring motif of the *rito* [rite], which Renello has rightly linked not just to the poem's central motif of death (in association with which the rite becomes a funeral rite), but also with that of factory labor, "The oppressive and harmful rite of factory labor."[164] Balestrini is explicit about what is at stake in this struggle. Not only is it a confrontation between "youth on one side power on the other," but, more generally, it exemplifies a project of communist liberation, "the universe of use values that confronts the factory and production."[165]

The motif of the patchwork quilt is associated, then, with the theme of labor autonomy, that is, with Tronti's *strategia del rifiuto* and the emergence of a new form of socio-political subjectivity. This is all the more suggestive given that precisely the same association can be found in the extended meditation on social and political space that is the penultimate chapter of *A Thousand Plateaus,* the celebrated collaborative work by Deleuze and Guattari published, like *Blackout*, in 1980.[166] In *A Thousand Plateaus,* Deleuze and Guattari seize on a distinction between smoothness and striation first drawn by the composer Pierre Boulez. They develop a theory of the segmentarity of socio-political space that closes with an analysis of those nomadic subjects that transform the measured and rationally structured space of capitalism into a smooth space: a space of autonomous and unpredictable movement—the space of the political event, or of revolution.[167]

One could easily formulate an interpretation of *Blackout* based entirely on the distinction between smooth and striated space. It is clear for example that the poem's first section, which opens with the description of a landscape and ends with an image of Manhattan, could be read in terms of a transition from smooth to striated space. Uncultivated landscapes such as mountain ranges are prime examples of smooth space, analogous to the deserts and oceans discussed by Deleuze and Guattari, and Manhattan is perhaps the world's most obviously striated urban space. Similarly, the description of the New York blackout clearly suggests an erasure of the city's striation, that is, a transformation of the city from a striated into a smooth space. Deleuze and Guattari emphasize that smooth and striated space should not be conceived of in absolute terms, as smooth space is constantly being transformed into striated space, and vice versa.

While a comprehensive exploration of the convergences between *Blackout* and the theory of smooth and striated space would be well worth undertaking, it will be best to focus here on what Deleuze and Guattari have to say about patchwork. The penultimate chapter of *A Thousand Plateaus* opens, like *Blackout*, with the photograph of a patchwork quilt. After a general discussion of the distinction between smooth and striated space, Deleuze and Guattari discuss various examples of these two kinds of space. They begin by discussing different kinds of cloth. Ordinary cloth patterns, based on a horizontal and vertical or grid-like division, are prime examples of striated space, and evoke all the socio-political connotations of such space. (Deleuze and Guattari cite Plato's association of the art of weaving with the art of governance.) The development of the patchwork quilt following European migration to North America—a process of flight, exit, or political defection, tied to the emergence of a new nomadic subject—is interpreted by Deleuze and Guattari as the invention of a kind of "*anti-tissu.*"[168] In the patchwork quilt, the striated space of the ordinary cloth is converted into a form of smooth space. The emergence of this new smooth space is directly linked to the existence of a form of collectivity that is autonomous in the sense of not being governed by the logic of capitalist production—namely, the collectivity of the quilting parties organized by female immigrants.

Whether Balestrini was aware of this theory when he wrote *Blackout* remains an open question. (He may well have been, given that both Deleuze and Guattari socialized with the Italian activists that escaped to France in 1979.) There is no doubt, however, that the Swiss-born autonomist Christian Marazzi has thought extensively about the discussion of patchwork found in *A Thousand Plateaus;* he refers explicitly to it in the second chapter of his 1998 publication *E il denaro va: esodo e rivoluzione dei mercati finanziari.*[169] This chapter—whose title is "1979"—is devoted to the re-structuring of global financial markets that began that year, following the adoption of the neo-liberal economic policies of Milton Friedman by the US Federal Reserve. In the economic theory of Marazzi, 1979 is associated with the rejection of Fordist and Keynesian economic policies and the constitution of a global post-Fordist economic regime. Marazzi compares this watershed to the beginning of the industrial revolution in England, arguing—very much in the spirit of *operaismo*—that global capital was constrained, by a prolonged and generalized refusal of Fordist factory labor as well as by an unprecedented rise in consumer spending, to radically transform itself. In other words, 1979 marked the final collapse of the Fordist system of production and its corollary institutions of welfare and collective bargaining, brought about by the struggles—in Italy and elsewhere—of the *operaio massa,* and by the emergence of new socio-political subjects whose needs and demands could no longer be governed by the mechanisms of an economic order inherited from the period before 1968. Seen from a global perspective, the repression of Italian autonomist Marxism reveals itself as occurring within the larger context of an epochal process of economic re-structuring induced by the struggles of labor.

It was in 1979 that the US Federal Reserve set out to rein in the inflation that had resulted from a dramatic increase in consumer spending.[170] The new president of the Federal Reserve, Paul Volker, chose to reduce inflation by raising interest rates and limiting the supply of money. To his surprise, inflation remained high as consumers simply made use of new forms of consumer credit (such as credit cards). Only when President Carter introduced a set of harsh credit regulations was there a reduction of consumer spending. The high interest rates set by the Federal Reserve began dramatically affecting private debt, and purchasing power was effectively curbed. Yet the situation was far from under control. The reduction in consumer spending proved so dramatic that Volker found himself faced with the threat of an economic crisis. He was constrained to reverse his previous policy by dramatically lowering interest rates (from 20% to 8% in the space of three months). There followed a new explosion of consumer purchases.

What had happened? On Marazzi's interpretation, the Federal Reserve had been forced to take notice of a new and ungovernable politico-economic subject: a working class that rejected the Fordist work ethic and refused to renounce the needs that had emerged during the era of post-war prosperity. Marazzi compares the events of 1979 in the USA to the explosion in the purchasing power of the working class that followed the dramatic fall in European cotton prices in 1842. This period had ushered in a joyful increase in the self-confidence of European workers, a small-scale cultural revolution that saw the drab garb of the pre-1842 worker replaced by a proliferation of colourful and often elaborately ornamented clothes, completely transforming the appearance of the major cities. Marazzi insists on the political significance of this event:

> In its own way, the revolution in cotton prices prepared the revolution of 1848, transforming the consciousness of the people whose real wages had hitherto constrained them to generate nothing but their own death. From that moment onward, labor consumerism will express the refusal of humiliating work and of that sound of machines "that one never gets used to," because one never gets used to not being able to dream.[171]

Marazzi develops these *operaista* themes throughout the rest of the chapter, insisting repeatedly on capitalism's dependence on labor's purchasing power. He cites the proliferation of the so-called "Economats" in the USA of the 19th century: stores where workers could use coupons to purchase the commodities they produced. A similar system, that of the so-called "credit bureaus," would later be implemented by the major automobile corporations, such as Ford. Yet the most interesting example, Marazzi insists, is that of the Singer Sewing Machine Company introducing payment by rates or so-called "hire-purchase" in 1850. As Marazzi says: "It can't go unobserved that it was the sewing machine that inspired the first rational forms of consumer credit."[172]

The widespread introduction of the Singer sewing machine, made possible by the system of hire-purchase, announced the rise of Fordism and the destruction of the autonomous collective space of the quilting party: "The sewing machine's entry into the private family space destroys the public space of those women's collectives that constituted themselves around the activity of weaving in America."[173] Just as "temporally segmented payment by rates corresponds perfectly to a mode of production segmented in space,"[174] the displacement of the quilt by the fabric sown on the Singer machine was co-terminous with the destruction, by the emergent Fordist system of production, of one of those autonomous socio-political spaces that Louis Althusser was fond of calling *"ilôts de comunisme"* [islands of communism].[175]

For Marazzi as for Deleuze and Guattari, the patchwork quilt is evocative of "informal and playful moments of cooperation,"[176] like Balestrini's "carpet of shoulders heads and arms that seems to move wavelike under gusts of wind."[177] The patchwork quilt represents a radical alternative to the striated space of Fordist factory labor:

> The *patchwork* is an amorphous, informal space, a place where one produces while communicating and communicates while producing, a temporal space where communication and the collective act of weaving coincide, such that the final product assumes a "crazy," anomalous, unforeseeable form, entirely different from other forms of fabric production (such as knitting), which require a disciplined and individualist organization of labor.[178]

Communication, collectivity, transformation and unpredictability—Marazzi's interpretation of the patchwork motif accords perfectly with the portrayal of the Movement of 1977 in the first section of *Blackout* (whose title is precisely "Trasformazione").[179]

The analogy goes further. *Blackout* is not simply a celebration of the Movement, but also a lament on its violent repression—an extended "metaphor of death," in Renello's words.[180] In much the same way, Marazzi insists that the disappearance of the quilting party—and, more generally, of the autonomous social spaces associated with it—was not effected by purely economic means, but by material violence:

> In the United States, the civil war of 1861-1865 will mark the definitive transition to the industrialization of the agricultural sector, necessary for eliminating the margins of self-sufficiency that working class families guarded jealously alongside their factory labor. The great cotton plantations cultivated by slaves were transformed, after the civil war, into modern-day enterprises. Behind consumer credit and Singer's hire-purchase system lies the story of the women and African slaves at the dawn of the Fordist revolution.[181]

Here as in *Blackout*, the patchwork cloth is an emblem of *autonomia* and *autovalorizzazione*. Like Balestrini, Marazzi also invokes the motif of flight or exit (the patchwork quilt is a cultural phenomenon historically linked to migration), the theme of a struggle between Fordist production and Althusserian "islands of communism," and images of bloody defeat. In other words, the motif of patchwork as used by Balestrini concords fully with its evocation both by Deleuze and Guattari and by Marazzi.

It is by considering its function in the works of Deleuze, Guattari, and Marazzi that one becomes alert to the richness and complexity of the patchwork motif. The reader alert to this richness discovers in the peculiar image that opens *Blackout*—the image of the patchwork quilt—the full spectrum of themes that the poem will go on to explore: joyful cooperation, labor autonomy, violent repression. Only an overhasty interpretation will see in Balestrini's scheme of composition an example of a repressively structured or striated space. Derived from the pattern of the patchwork quilt, the scheme contains—as a kind of coded message—a vindication of the joyful processes of *autovalorizzazione* that provided the ultimate impetus for the state repression of 1979: "the FIAT bosses have never seen the workers laugh and it makes them mad as hell."[182] Fundamentally—that is, on the level of form—*Blackout* is not just an extended "metaphor of death,"[183] but also an unrepentant vindication of what Balestrini has elsewhere described as "a period that was yes hard and tense but that was also and most of all a period of vitality and joy and intelligence and passion."[184]

CHAPTER SIX

MARISA GIORGI

USEPPE'S STATE OF EXCEPTION IN ELSA MORANTE'S *HISTORY*

A state of exception can be described as a period of time in which the laws of Society[185] are suspended due to extenuating circumstances, often as a result of war. Such is the case with Elsa Morante's novel, *History: A novel*[186] (1974). It is set during and after World War II, and so the entirety of the novel takes place in a state of exception. This novel is of further interest regarding this topic because it is placed temporarily and spatially within History; that is, each chapter is introduced by actual historical events that transpire concurrently with the characters' lives and the narrative within. To that point, the characters exist in a contemporary Rome. The locations in the book are real and have historical value in delineating both the novel's history and our History.

History follows the various characters as they try and carry on normal lives; however throughout the pages we learn of their personal tragedies caused by History. The novel recounts the personal history of a widow by the name of Ida Raimundo Mancuso, living in Rome during and after World War II. Throughout her story she and many others are afflicted by fear and are, of course, forced to live in a state of exception as a direct result of World War II. However, the most poignant case of both scandal and exclusion is that of the smallest and most innocent character, Ida's infant son, Giuseppe Angiolino Felice, known simply as, Useppe.

Useppe's character is particularly interesting because he is the only one born during a state of exception, but in Useppe's case there are many levels or "states" of exception—social, historical and physical, which help form his story and experience. Useppe is conceived when a German soldier rapes Ida (social); during this act of violence Ida faints, and is therefore unconscious during the subsequent conception of Useppe (physical). This sequence of events foreshadows the life of the exceptional child, Useppe.

Useppe's inability to speak Italian is one of the primary factors that keeps him removed from Society. Others include his uncanny connection to the animal world and his ability to communicate with it, as well as his pure innocence. All of these can be described as "fantastic" or even exceptional qualities. Gregory Lucente notes these qualities and compares Useppe to an angel, underlining his inherent goodness:

> The child's faculties of imagination and wonderment portrayed in the novel are clearly distinct from those of others, as though Useppe were indeed the lost angel of light caught alone in the snare of History's darkness.[187]

Useppe's purity and happiness separate him from the world of evil by which he is surrounded, enabling him to remain apart from it. At the time of his tragic death, he cannot even pronounce his own name correctly, let alone, speak Italian, further underlining his exclusion from Society.

Scared and ashamed, Ida attempts to hide her pregnancy with Useppe from everyone. Fearing what others will think of her, she closets herself from society,[188] concealing the pregnancy even from her own son, Nino—in fact, especially from Nino. Ida is so preoccupied with others' opinions of her that she does not realize that she is hiding from a Society that functionally no longer exists, which is now merely a memory, due to the invasion and bombing of Rome. She is living in a state of exception, but at some level is unable to fully accept it, and is therefore clinging to conventional mores and expectations of behavior, afraid someone will discover her secret. Through her successful cover-up of the pregnancy, Ida, once again, foreshadows the all too brief life of Useppe. As he was kept hidden from society in-utero, Useppe will remain removed from society for the duration of his life, denied physical participation as an object born out of shame, fear and guilt.

Useppe manages to communicate with his human family through a language he creates practically on his own. His language is a mix of Italian, Roman dialect, and baby talk. However, it is not merely baby talk; Elsa Morante did not create a separate language for Useppe so that he would seem "cute." His lexicon serves an important role in the novel, that is, to underline his separation from the rest of Society. A perfect example is the fact that he calls himself Useppe. He was incapable, at first, of pronouncing Giuseppe, and Nino happened to like the nickname. This mispronunciation of his name that is accepted by everyone only further contributes to his difficulties with the Italian language, thus decreasing the possibility that he will be able to participate in Society.

At a certain point, even Nino, who nicknamed him Useppe thinks that he is too mature to still be speaking like a baby and tells Useppe to pronounce his "r"s correctly, at which point he also begins to pronounce his "s"s like a small child again. These corrections are coming from Nino, who even in that very moment is speaking Roman dialect and has taught Useppe curse words in the past. Nino now expects Useppe to speak correct Italian, or at least pronounce words correctly, even though Useppe, unlike Nino, was born during a state of exception and therefore, has never attended school or had the means to learn to speak proper Italian. The main difference between Nino and Useppe, regarding language, and the fact that neither one of them actually speaks proper Italian, is that Nino is capable of speaking Italian well, but chooses not to. Useppe, on the other hand, is not capable of speaking Italian, neither correctly nor fluently, symbolizing his displacement from Society. Nino, however, realizes that it is not normal for a boy of Useppe's age (five) to still be speaking like a baby. He also notices that in Useppe's eyes, there is something different, something that was never there before. Perhaps what Nino sees in Useppe's eyes is fear, or even gradual acknowledgement of his special state.

It is thematically significant that Ida hates the fact that Nino is constantly speaking Roman dialect instead of standard Italian. Ida, ever the teacher, does not want her son speaking such a low form of Italian, and fears that as a result, others will think that Nino is not educated and also fears that Useppe will pick up this bad habit, never mind the fact that he can't speak Italian at all. Again, she conforms to social standards (imaginary or self-imposed) that have become obsolete or irrelevant since the suspension of normal Society by the state of exception caused by the war. However, Nino's response is very interesting not only because he speaks in dialect, but because it speaks to the theme of language in general, underlining its importance in the novel. Nino proclaims in perfect dialect, that: "We live in Rome, and we talk Romano! When we're in Paris (where I plan to go soon, now that Paris is ours!) we'll talk Parisian! And when we're in Hong Kong, on our next crusade, we'll talk Konguese!"[189]

Nino, as opposed to Useppe, clearly operates within Society—or rather, embraces the codes and structures created by this exceptional state—identifying and, to a certain extent, even defining himself with a particular part of Society by intentionally speaking a specific form (Roman dialect) of Italian. At this point of the novel he consciously considers himself to be Roman, complete with Fascist ideals and growing adoration for Mussolini—naturally he would speak Roman. As the novel progresses, however, so does Nino, and seeing the error in his ways he joins the Partisans, though he does continue to speak Roman dialect instead of standard Italian.

Nino's views on language are intriguing and worth analyzing. Rather than speaking the language of a nation of people (Italian or French for example) he believes that one should speak dialect, which is by definition a language of a small society of people. Language either separates or unites a people, and in the case of dialects it unites a smaller group of people by removing them, linguistically, from the larger Society and placing them in a smaller society of their own. According to Giorgio Agamben, dialects are languages without sovereign states. Leaving all else aside for the moment, and based purely on

Useppe's language, he is twice removed from Society because the grammar he uses to string together his made up words, is not Italian grammar but the grammar of Roman dialect, those words that he did not make up himself are Roman dialect and do not exist in standard Italian. Thus, a normally unifying instrument of communication is not used as such, but rather as a sectarian tool that perpetuates the dissolution of society during a state of exception.

Ida, however, does not ever seem concerned by the fact that Useppe is not learning to speak proper Italian, she is more concerned with the fact that he is picking up curse words from Nino than the fact that he has a very limited vocabulary for his age. Again, her concerns are molded by the assumed standards of a Society long since corrupted. She neither seems terribly concerned by the fact that since Useppe is escaping from school everyday, he is not learning to read or write Italian. As a product of the war, in every sense of the word, Useppe is not entitled to the same rights as most children, such as Nino, who was raised in a period of relative peace. Ida's top priority is survival, both her own and Useppe's. Ida and Useppe rely on each other for their own survival. Obviously, Useppe is too young to be able to survive on his own, but it is doubtful that Ida would have survived the war had it not been for Useppe's dependency on her. Knowing that her child's survival relied on her own survival is most likely what kept Ida "fighting" through the hardships she encountered, and perhaps of even greater concern, prevented her from turning herself into the Gestapo as a Jew. It is made very clear at certain points in the novel, that Ida has a great sense of guilt over having escaped the racial laws and persecutions, and survived, while so many others just like her perished. Her guilt is a result of an adherence to the practices and restraints of pre-war Society.

The fact that Useppe understands the animal language and therefore has a special bond with the animal world removes him even further from Society, placing him somewhere between our world and the animal world; even from the moment of his birth, it is not clear to which Useppe belongs. He is immediately compared to a small lamb "born last and forgotten in the straw."[190] These ties to the animal world are more thoroughly forged at home as he spends most of his days in the care of the family dog, Blitz. He and Blitz develop a special relationship communicating perfectly with each other, even before Useppe is capable of communicating with his own family.

Morante even goes as far as to explain how Useppe learns to speak and understand the language of dogs. The narrator tells us that each sound Useppe made was perfectly comprehensible to Blitz, and that they would spend hours playing and conversing together on the floor, a sign that Useppe may very well be more closely connected to the animal world than the human world. In his short life it is very likely that Useppe actually spends more time with dogs than he does with humans. From his birth until the bombing of Rome he spends his days home alone with Blitz, while Ida is teaching and Nino is roaming the streets. After the bombing of Rome, Ida and Useppe find refuge in a large room, referred to as the *stanzone* outside of Rome in Pietralata. It is here that Useppe will spend the most time with other humans, as Blitz was killed when the Raimundo home was destroyed in the bombing. Eventually, Bella, Nino's dog left in Useppe's care, becomes his new companion and surrogate mother. It is no wonder that Useppe never learns to speak proper Italian, but communicates perfectly with his canine friends; after all, his first words did not belong to a human language, but rather that of dogs, literally his mother tongue. Perhaps it is through Useppe's animal instinct that he subconsciously realizes that if he denies human contact or dialogue he does not have to belong to this world that so clearly terrifies his mother: Society. Since communication is the clearest sign that one participates in Society, Useppe retreats to his animal world, taking steps backwards in his pronunciation, and the language learning process.

Another key theme stemming from this fear of Society and contributing significantly to Useppe's exclusion from it is his misunderstanding of death. At the *stanzone* in Pietralata one of Ida and Useppe's fellow refugees, Giuseppe Secondo (or to Useppe, Eppetondo), keeps two small canaries. While on a trip to visit the Partisan camp with Nino, Useppe thinks that he sees the canaries. However, they had recently died, and therefore the birds that Useppe sees at the Partisan camp cannot be the same from the *stanzone.* However, he hears the birds singing a song: "*It's a joke, a joke, it's all a joke.*"[191] Not only does this sequence clarify that Useppe understands the language of birds as well as dogs, but it also serves to show that Useppe refutes the death of the birds entirely. So that there is no misunderstanding on the part of the reader, the narrator quickly describes Useppe's misunderstanding of the tragic event: "Obviously the big room's two songsters, this morning, as soon as they were cured of their sanguinary illness, had flown here..."[192] Useppe clearly has the image of the dead, bloody canaries in his head, and yet wants to believe that the birds he sees at the camp are the same. The song that Useppe hears the birds singing is wholly symbolic and has a direct correlation with his refusal of death; it refers to the actual death of the canaries, as well as death in general. What Useppe understands from the canaries' song is that it is all a big misunderstanding, a joke. They weren't really dead when Useppe saw them last, they were merely injured and have followed him and Nino all the way to prove it.

Useppe lives in his own Utopia where death does not exist and animals and humans are not separated by language; he neither understands nor accepts the laws of Society. Nor does he consciously refuse them. He exists in a world of his natural making, on his terms. There was never any other choice for him. He believes that Blitz simply flew away, as he was told by a kind, elderly woman the day of the bombing. Useppe's understanding of death is that when something "flies away", like Blitz, he will never see it again. Thus, his only rational response is to deny the fact of death completely. Useppe's entire existence occurs in a time in which the laws of Society are suspended. Therefore he is not obliged to accept the most fundamental laws of life itself; not even death.

Near the end of his short life Useppe hears the same song once again, this time while he is with his new friend, Scimó, who naturally does not hear the song. It is not by chance that Useppe hears this song again, so close to his own death. He is in denial of his own illness, epilepsy, and his own impending death. Useppe mentions the song to his friend, Scimó, who in turn, asks Useppe what song he is talking about. At this point Useppe becomes embarrassed; he does not know how to explain his special relationship with the animal world. At a certain level Useppe knows that he is different and therefore, much of what he hears and does is not accepted by Society. He does not want to tell Scimó the truth for fear of his reaction; not knowing how to respond to Scimó's question, he simply stares at his feet repeating the words of the song.

Useppe's encounters with Scimó in the novel are noteworthy because they are among the few instances in which we see Useppe interact with someone who is more or less a peer. Granted, Scimó is quite a bit older than Useppe, but he is a friend that Useppe made on his own. Scimó's presence in the novel seems to underline, once again, Useppe's purity and innocence and to reiterate that there is no place in such a corrupt society for a being with those qualities. Useppe is fascinated by Scimó, simply because he has never known anyone like him, and because he introduces Useppe to a world he has never seen before; bragging about his American cigarettes, and his Australian tank top, that he gets from the local queens, giving Useppe a kind of sneak peak into the corrupt world that everyone, except he participates in. Scimó and his delinquent friends are representative of evil in the world and examples of how History has corrupted Society's youth. Scimó is a threat to Usepppe's pure innocence; he is Temptation, showing him glimpses of his world of danger and excitement. Useppe, however, does not realize this, only his canine mother, Bella, recognizes Scimó for the threat that he is. In fact, she is somewhat wary of Useppe's new friend and extremely attentive when he is around. In one particular scene in which the two boys are hanging out, Scimó begins to raise his voice, which Bella interprets as aggression towards Useppe. In an effort to calm him down and defuse the situation, Bella immediately throws herself toward Scimó's neck, licking him across the face and giving him a painless nip or two on his ears. Scimó sees this action as an accusation and feels threatened by Bella, but at the same time, the point has been made self-evident to Scimó, that she is Useppe's protector. She knows that Scimó is no good for Useppe and will only introduce him to a world of evil and corrupt his innocence; an innocence that sets him apart and ultimately protects him from everyone and everything else. It is in the boys' reactions to Bella's protectiveness of Useppe that we see the manifestation of the age-old battle between good and evil. Not knowing how else to react, the two boys simply smile at each other, Scimò's smile showing a mouthful of dark stained teeth, already in bad condition, while Useppe's smile instead, shows off his soft, milk-white baby's teeth. This image of the two boys demonstrates the effects History has already had on Scimò, affirming the notion that the characters of the novel are generally good, and only as a result of History are they corrupted.

The fact that Useppe has both a human mother and a canine mother reinforces the idea that he is an outcast. Not fully belonging to either world, he truly has one foot in the animal world and one foot in the human world. However, in some respects Useppe is more closely tied to the world of animals than that of humans. As the critic, Concetta D'Angelia notes,

> Useppe is ashamed of his sickness he keeps himself segregated from others, just as animals do when they are sick, without ever finding the words or gestures to tell anyone...the impossibility of communicating using normal means of language...the impossibility of recounting the horror.[193]

Once again, at the root of the problem is the fact that Useppe is extremely limited in what he can communicate to other humans. He can, however, communicate whatever he wants to Bella, yet he refuses to speak of his illness. Even with her, his canine mother, he is ashamed. If his human mother, Ida, had not witnessed one of Useppe's epileptic attacks, she may never have known that he was even sick. Like a wounded animal, Useppe is not capable of understanding or explaining his illness.

A very important aspect of Useppe's particular lexicon is his poetry. Much of Useppe's poetry is influenced by his own experiences, even those that he may not remember. For example, bits of the same nursery rhymes that Ida's anarchist father would sing to her, and in turn Ida would sing to both Nino and Useppe, appear in his poetry. Useppe inherits more than just a name and nursery rhymes from his grandfather: he also inherits his grandfather's connection to the animal world, the world in general, and his anarchism. Useppe, like his grandfather is an anarchist, this is made evident by his complete refusal of Society's rules. It is quite fitting that the memory and legacy of Giuseppe Raimundo lives on in his grandson and namesake.

As a poet, what makes Useppe special is the fact that he is an illiterate child capable of creating beautiful, if simple poetry. As noted below by Gregory Lucente, it is clear that Useppe's talent for poetry is inherent:

> The transformation that things undergo in Useppe's linguistic imagination serves to heighten similarities by ignoring basic differences and by interchanging essences and attributes...At the same time, his poems are not 'fictional' or feigned, since they represent real, direct perception of his world...[194]

Lucente's comment that Useppe ignores basic differences is noteworthy because it further underlines the fact that for Useppe the lines of separation between animals and humans are blurred. Nothing is more natural for Useppe than poetry. This idea is reinforced by the fact that in his poetry, he correctly pronounces the majority of words that he usually pronounces like a baby. However, he has no interest in writing his poems, nor does he have any interest in the written word at all.

The fact that Useppe refuses to go to school, running home everyday, is evidence of his total refusal of the rules and laws of Society. He knows that his place is not at school, amongst relatively normal children where his exceptional qualities or abnormalities will be exposed. Useppe does not want to participate in a Society to which he so clearly does not belong, nor can he. So he runs to where he feels safest, not to his mother who is another teacher at that same school, and thus part of Society, but to his canine mother, Bella.

The death of Nino, the only human death that Useppe has to ever deal with, leaves a large void in his life. Useppe, of course, does not understand that Nino has died; he simply knows that like Blitz, he will never see Nino again. In an attempt to fill the void left by Nino, Useppe looks to Nino's best friend, Davide Segre, the only human with whom Useppe ever shares his poetry. As Nino's best friend, Davide feels some kind of responsibility to befriend Useppe, but is incapable and unwilling to be the father figure that Nino was, despite all his shortcomings. Another possible reason why Useppe is attracted to Davide could be that Useppe recognizes in Davide his passion for poetry, a form of purity that he can relate to. If it were not for the relationship that Useppe develops with Davide, he would not have the opportunity to share his poetry with anyone, including the reader. It is a direct result of Useppe's relationship with Davide that we understand that he is a child poet and why it is necessary for the development of his character.

Upon discovering that Useppe is also a poet, Davide naturally asks if he can read some of his poems and "as usual in moments of emotion or confusion, Useppe lapsed into his erroneous, abbreviated baby's utterances"[195] stating unequivocally and almost angrily, that he never writes his poems, but that he simply thinks them up and then he recites them, usually only to Bella, but on this special occasion, to Davide as well. The omniscient narrator tells us that the subject of the written word, is an emotional and confusing one for Useppe because unlike when he is reciting his poetry he begins mispronouncing his words. Thus, Useppe refuses to allow the naturalness and innocence of his poetry to be constrained by the approved modes of expressions.

As the poets of the novel, Davide and Useppe could not be any more different, in their personalities or in their poetic styles, although there remains a direct correlation between both. Useppe's poems stem from his pure happiness, which is in turn, a direct result of his innocence, and his inherent incorruptibility. However, like a true poet, Useppe discusses in his poetry his life experiences, nature, and even uses as a source of inspiration, some of the saddest moments in his life. It is not by coincidence that in the following excerpt Useppe speaks of the canaries from the stanzone:

> The fish like canaries. And they fly away.
> And the leaves like wings. And they fly away.
> And the horse like a flag.
> And he flys away.[196]

It is obvious that Useppe is referring to death in this poem. From the moment he is told that Blitz flew away: he is curious as to what other things "fly away." In fact, it is one of his primary concerns before he accepts Bella from Nino; he wants to know if she too, like Blitz will fly away.

In a later conversation with Davide about death and Hell, Useppe affirms, albeit in his own language mixed with Roman dialect, that Hell does not exist, justifying his position through a logical argument. According to Useppe, animals fly away, and since he does not distinguish between the human and animal worlds, he believes that people also fly away. Death does not exist in Useppe's world and if there is no death, then there is no Hell. It is important to note that throughout this discussion, although his vocabulary and grammar are lacking, Useppe's pronunciation, as in his poetry recitations, is perfect. This is the only instance in which Useppe clearly states and defends his infantile understanding of death, however his argument, albeit erroneous, is logical. Morante uses this conversation with Davide as a tool to help the reader understand that Useppe is not an idiot child, but rather to demonstrate the effects History has had on him and his relationship with Society. Useppe can never be a part of Society, but will remain happily in his own Utopia where death, sadness, and the evils of Society are non-factors.

As the only other poet in the novel Davide understands Useppe in a way that no one else can; he is the only person in the novel that seems to be aware of Useppe's special status and who recognizes Useppe's pure innocence and happiness. Perhaps it is because they are both poets and attempt to articulate the unspoken that they share a special bond and have a certain wordless understanding. He is the only adult character that treats Useppe as an equal, in the way he addresses him, and in the conversations he has with him; they are not the normal conversations that an adult has with a five year old. It is through Davide that we learn absolutely and unequivocally that Useppe does not belong to society, stating in a conversation with Useppe: "You're the happiest creature in the world. Always, every time I've seen you, I've thought that, since the first day I met you...you're too pretty for this world; you don't belong here. What do they say? *Happiness is not of this world...*"[197] implying that neither is Useppe. When this conversation takes place, we are nearing the end of the novel and although Davide is speaking to Useppe, his words are for the reader's benefit. Useppe is aware at some level that he is different, and does not need to be told so. It is Morante's way of signaling to the reader Useppe's importance in *History.*

During his brief time on Earth, poetry is what saves Useppe from being forced into a Society to which he does not belong, but ultimately not even poetry can save him from History's intervening actions. Through his poetry he proves that he is not an idiot child, he willingly does not want to partake in a Society so corrupt and evil. As a result of his poems, he is granted immortality, something History cannot take away from him, but must grant him in spite of itself. Useppe's poems are born out of his purity, as opposed to the contrivance of Davide's poems, and in this way Useppe saves poetry.

Useppe is the soul of the novel; his story is the essence of *History.* It is, ironically enough, his contribution to Society, the very thing that he cannot and will not be a part of. His story, however, is only made known to us as a result of his poetry, so in effect he contributes to Society on his own terms, without ever conforming to the accepted forms of expression. Useppe refutes the written word partly because he is illiterate and partly because at some level he is aware of his state of exception and therefore, is not obligated to accept the doctrines of Society.

Useppe is the greatest tragedy of the personal history of the Raimundo family. He is a product of war—an innocent child born out of violence whose entire existence can be attributed to the scandal that is World War II. At the root of Useppe's exceptional state is language. His lexicon—his poetry and ability to speak and understand animal languages—is what separates him most poignantly from Society. The language Useppe uses to communicate with other people is not an accepted form of verbal expression—that is, it is neither a language nor a dialect, but a language of his own invention. Compounding the difficult situation, he cannot write or read, and therefore cannot effectively communicate with Society. Instead, he creates his own world on his own terms, communicating only with his family, animals and the occasional friend. Ultimately it is Useppe's misunderstanding of language and death that sanction his exclusion from Society and pre-determine his tragic end.

Chapter Seven

Chiara Sartori

Trieste, Borderline Identity

Does it make sense today to speak of a geographically delineated entity when Italy's national identity stands in crisis? We are so afraid of "the Other" because we do not know ourselves anymore. Here, precisely, lies the reason why today more than ever it is important to heed debates surrounding minorities and identities.

In the contemporary culture of difference, the void left from the dissolution of absolutisms and essential truths can lead even to one's personal and social identity being torn apart. This cannot but make the problem of identity ever more present, confronted now not only from a philosophical, ethical and political point of view, but also from the perspective of the social sciences. The anthropologist Friedrick Barth in 1969 called into question every definition of identity as static, confined within definite boundaries.[198] Edward Said in 1978 invited us to look at eastern cultures as a mirror and "dark alter ego" of western cultures.[199] Diversity has become the privileged perspective from which to approach discourses about "the self." Galimberti, in his work *Psyche and Techne,* writes that in this era of technology, "the recognition of personal identity has as its implication the recognition of the alterity of the other because each one is itself only if it is not the other from whom one differentiates his or herself."[200]

For Galimberti, identity today derives from the role we play, and the relation and socialization that that role entails.[201] Francesco Remotti, in his essay *Contro l'identità*, published in 1996, further sees a danger in alterity. He ardently affirms the relation between the modern reclamation of identity and the affirmation of the individual and collective selves to the detriment of the other: "It is in the self-interest, therefore, of the identity to smash, to make disappear from the horizon alterity."[202] In 2002, Remotti also highlights strength, weaknesses and fundamental elusiveness of a concept of identity that, "is from time to time invented, constructed, imagined," in constant defence against the threat of alterity.[203] Every analysis of the other is necessarily tormented, because relations with diversity themselves are both tormented and dynamic. Today it makes sense to speak of Orientalism because there has been, in the Western, a progressive and dramatic weakening of interest in our own history, and origins. After the fall of the Berlin Wall in 1989 the West found itself having to face reality: identities are not formed by violence, nor are they created ad hoc with artificial boundaries. Human dynamics are far too complex for this. Thus, the present debate on the problem of Italian national identity is influenced by its current social and political condition. In the last few years numerous publications have investigated of Italians' sense of national membership. The *leitmotif* of these texts is the difficulty in finding a common characteristic that defines "Italianicity." Remo Bodei does not see a unifying worldview among Italians because, "in the face of contemporary pluralism and in the loss of the historical origins of the philosophies of difference there is no room for strong and singularly interpreted values."[204] Abruzzese therefore outlines the conflict between cultural and political identity and shows how our concept of "Italianicity" lacks self-coherence. Most probably Italy herself is explainable only as the sum of her subjectivity, and when Banti, Raimondi, Dalla Loggia and Bruno try to define our country anthropologically and culturally they succeed only in summarizing particularisms and in identifying influencing factors, but not in arriving at true and holistic conclusions. They all cite diverse heritages (the Roman tradition and the Catholic Church, the Risorgimento, Fascism and Italian-style consumerism) but they are careful to eschew unifying or absolute definitions (Italians, for instance, are not all Catholics, fascists or communists, much less patriots). It seems, therefore, that "Italy" emerges from the collision of these factors than from the assimilation of them. Discussions of patriotism are thus confined to the period of the Risorgimento and to the patriotic literature of the nineteenth century. Italy, with her contradictions and plural identities is without a doubt the European state that has the most trouble finding a strong unifying National identity. For an Italian to feel love for his country, he must go abroad, or watch the World Cup, a metaphor for a territorial war. Certainly these difficulties are not new, even Giacomo Leopardi pondered Italian pluralism. That which to me seems most novel is the cultural climate in which the question currently arises. "Weak thought," relativism, and the challenges of globalization preclude, rather than further, the discussions of identity.[205] Trieste is a lens through which to view the development of modern research on a strong identity. Trieste, before other Italian cities, confronted psychoanalysis and multiculturalism.[206] Trieste's conception of "Italianicity" has always accounted for Slavs, Austrians, Greeks and Jews, and it is because of this, perhaps, that in this city a response to the modern-day crisis of identity might be found. He who must search every day for his own identity does not turn to literature for pleasure, but for answers: "The 'anti-literary' attitude amongst the people of Trieste can be explained by the attitude of men who ask of writing not beauty but truth, because for them to write means to acquire an identity not just as writers, but also as a group."[207] It is not by choice that Trieste is the city of Saba and Svevo and that Friuli is home to Tomizza; it is not by accident that Trieste was the first place in Italy to come to know German romantic philosophy and literature through the translation of young contributors to *La Voce.*[208] In its existence as a land of boundaries, of meeting and clashing between alterity and difference, this city has had to continually reinvent and redefine itself, always already dialectically recreating itself. Even Slataper in 1909 decried on the pages of *La Voce* that, "Trieste does not have cultural traditions."[209] In fact, as Guagnini asserts in the first pages of his contribution to Apih's essay,

> Apart from some recent efforts, the history and literature of Trieste has been *prevailingly* identified with Italian history and literature," thus attributing to the Triestine condition certain typical characteristics that while pertaining to Triestine literature, are not exclusive to it.[210]

Often one forgets that, during Italian literature's highly productive era in the nineteenth and twentieth centuries, in Trieste both German and Slovene literatures flourished as well because "if not for other reasons than the diffusion of in the languages, institutions, and culture Italians, Slovenes and Germans would be able to conserve and to strengthen their presence in Trieste."[211] Slataper himself, Slavic by birth, German by education and Italian by tongue, finds in poetry the possibility of resolving the contradictions of his identity. Trieste is not, like Fiume, poly-lingual and poly-cultural, but the relationship between Italians and Slovenes is one that is, "before conflict, of separation."[212] There are few points of contact between the two ethnic groups, and those what exist are often unidirectional. The Slovenes know the Italian language, but the Italians do not know the Slovenian one: "Trieste's multinationality derives from the dimension in which diverse cultures come into contact with each other…in an environment that is nonetheless essentially Italian."[213] Conventionally speaking, until the nineteenh century, Trieste almost did not have literature, but the Pitteris and Rinaldis are, for Ara and Magris "descendants of the Italians, whom they make their own and the tradition of whom they continued into later years."[214] Rossetti and Kandler, the two representatives of Istrian humanism, lack the particularness and originality of the subsequent generation. The same goes for the Germans Raab and Menzel, who are not even mentioned in the literature of their own countries, and for the Slovenes Koseski and Tuma, who remain largely unknown. Triestine literature's official birth date coincides with the publication of the great novels by Svevo, but we must not forget the generation of Triestine intellectuals that, at the beginning of the century, moved between Florence and Vienna, and found in these two respective languages and cultures, their own roots:

> The Triestine avant-garde that in the first decade of the twentieth century goes to study in Florence—Slataper, Giani e Carlo Stuparich, Spaini, Devescovi, Marin and many others—is also in search of a linguistic formation, of a perfected stylistic mastery of Italian that permits them to charter and develop their own culture.[215]

Florence, Vienna and Prague become in this period the three cities of culture for the young Triestines mediators of divergent identities. Trieste serves as the ideal vantage point from which to observe Europe. Trieste's mission should have been that of "mediation and cultural conciliation amongst Latin Germanic and Slavic groups."[216] From this perspective, we can see that for these writers, adopting Italianicity served political as well as linguistic ends.[217] *Fin de siècle* Trieste exuded an internationality unknown elsewhere in Italy: Triestines read not only Freud and Rilke, but also Hebbel and Ibsen, in Slataper's translation, and they were familiar with Kafka's Prague as interpreted for them by Spaini. The story of the young Triestine intellectuals at the early twentieth century, united by strong bonds of friendship, is the story of a dream and upon waking from this dream, Triestines found themselves among the ruins of Old Europe[218]. Black and white conceptions of Trieste crossed paths in the borderline authors: "In *Mio Carso* there are two souls, the one Italian, wearily in decline, and the other Slovene, ever vital."[219]

Svevo's illness, Saba's war, and Slataper's Carso also betray the two souls of a multiform city, united by a bourgeois and commercial purpose:

> Trieste is Italian. And it is an outlet of German interest. It must want a railway, two railways, that link it to Germany. And it must be thankful for the nurturing of the commerce, and for the people of mixed blood that those railways transport. It is the travails of these two natures that clash so as annihilate each other in turn: the commercial and the Italian. And Trieste cannot choke either of the two: it is its double soul: she (Trieste) would kill herself.[220]

To Svevo goes the credit of having identified Trieste as the ideal landscape in which to recount the preoccupations of the modern world. His novels's characters are heroes/anti-heroes of the contemporary condition. They are the sick that make of their sickness their strength, protagonists of that Nietzscheanism that the author perceives in himself: "only at the end, the author of *Zeno's Confessions* one realizes, with hesitant and incredulous happiness, that he is neither just a victim nor a mere product of that world which to him appeared to be the only possibility, but also a dissolver and destroyer of that world, a descendant."[221] Zeno in turn makes his sickness into the centre of his existence, and in this sense he is the prototype of the modern cosmopolitan, whose omphaloskepsis enables him to escape from the merry-go-round of globalization. Trieste, a city rich in stimuli and vitality, is pitiless and cruel to those who cannot keep pace.[222] If the identity of Trieste represented by Svevo becomes at once a paradigm and also a denunciation of post-modernism, then the two wars brought emphasis to the middle-European soul of this city. The fall of the Austro-Hungarian Empire signalled profound economic and social changes for the city. Slovenes, Italians, Austrians, Jews and Greeks had been united by common economic interests, and held together by maritime traffic and the intelligent politics of Maria Teresa, who had unified a diverse population under a single crown. The war reawakened ancient hatreds and appeased nationalisms. The Slovene *carsolino* Srecko Kosovel, Gambini, the *gradesi* Biagio and Falco Marin and above all Umberto Saba related the political and social ordeals the city must face.[223] While Saba universalized and transfigured the anguishing Triestine situation into a paradigm of the human condition, other writers towed on the particular issues facing the *giuliane* lands in communicate the European catastrophe.[224] The years of the post-war period are instead the years of Tomizza, who recounted the dramas of the exodus and of the Istrian situation, but they are also the years in which new *topoi* were created: "The *topos* of middle Europe substitutes for *topos* of Italianicity, all the more legitimate and all the more abused. Alongside of the historical revisionism of the movement to reunite those Italian territories to the "motherland" that were still subjects of Austria are not only studies of the genesis of the idea of Middle Europe and of Austro-Marxism, but also includes the cultural discovery of the Austro-Hungarian empire."[225] Austria and the Hapsburg Empire thus become the symbol of lost unity. The drama of the border, the diversity of Trieste, its being a *nowhere,* and the discourse of boundaries often find resolution only by revisiting past myths.[226] Contemporary literature, on the one hand, aims to underscore diversity and the tragedy of the border in the desperate search for Triestineness, which becomes itself a borderline identity and, on the other hand, attempts to merge with the middle European identity to which it belongs. The "contemporaneity" is not a synthesis, as Ara and Magris say, but just the opposite: rather than interaction, "it is a mere addition and heterogeneous alignment of irreducible presumptions and particularities in flight."[227] Here it is then that the city becomes once again a microcosm reflecting contemporary chaos.

What remains today of this tormented *nowhere?* What are the words and themes with which one narrates the border? *Microcosmi* was written in 1997, during the war that was bloodying the Balkans. Bosnia, Serbia and Kosovo were asserting borders and divisions, while Europe was refuting them. Like the Tommaseo, from whose tables Magris had started another long voyage, the sentimental and historical voyage of *Danubio, Microcosmi* departs from Caffe' San Marco. The café' is a privileged point of observation:

> Chess players love the café—it resembles a chessboard and one moves between its tables like a knight, making a series of right angles and often finding oneself, as in a game of snakes and ladders, back at square one...back at that table where one had studied for the German literature exam and now, many years later, one wrote or responded to yet another interview about Trieste, its *Mitteleuropa* culture and its decline, while not far away one son is correcting his degree dissertation and another, in the ending room, is playing cards.[228]

Magris's writing is at times free association and a dance of images; the temporal and emotional streams of consciousness cross each other not just in these passages but also throughout the novel. He mixes literary theory with narrative in works that, more than just novels are essays, manifestos of a condition (Triestineness – or better – middle European-ness at the end of the millennium) of which this author is, in the meantime, witness and prophet:

> Our identity is partly made up of places, of the streets where we have lived and left part of ourselves...Vienna is one of these places, in which I rediscover the familiar and well known, the enchantment of things which, like friendship and love, become ever fresher with time. This feeling of ease with Vienna may derive from the city's being a crossroads, a place of departures and returns, of people, both celebrated and obscure, whom history gathers together and then disperses, in the vagabond impermanence that is our destiny.[229]

Vienna is like Trieste, and the old Vienna is a "passage from goodbye to happiness."[230] Here we see why it is worth looking for traces of this same identity along the course of the Danube. The Danube is the long river which mixes diverse people, rather than being, like the Rhine, a mythic custodian of pure birth: "even since the *Song of the Niebelungs* the Rhine and the Danube have confronted and challenged each other. The Rhine is Siegfried, symbol of Germanic *virtus* and purity, the loyalty of the Niebelungs...The Danube is Pannonia, the kingdom of Attila, the Eastern, Asiatic tide..." [231] In these words there is the *distinguo* of the Triestine intellectuals that are most careful not to confuse Germany with Austria, a tendency to which not even Rumiz is immune since, having arrived at the Berlin station of Friedrichstrasse, can't but notice "different dresses, different biorhythms, different incomes. Different even in their speaking: classical German to eastern, Americanized German on the other hand."[232] In *Microcosmi,* Magris follows by explaining that "the Danube is Middle Europe German, Magyar, "Slavic," Roman, Jewish, polemically counter posed to the German *Reich.*" In fact, "Austrianicity is the art of flight, vagabonding, love of the reprieve in anticipation of a motherland that, as the

Schubert's wayfarer states, is always sought after, forecast, but never known:"[233] Austrian nomadism and the obsession for flight are trends of these authors of the end of the millennium. Unlike Svevo, detachment is no longer possible or sufficient. The only therapy for modernity is the search, the burning desire to reclaim one's roots. The border finds peace not in the annihilation of one or another culture, but in the attempt to find a common past, the outline of which serves as a standpoint from which to mediate diversity. Rumiz, who defines himself as a traveller, repeatedly consecrates Trieste both as a city of departure and as a point of arrival. About the Danube he explains that,

> A voyage on the Danube can begin well in Trieste. Just as it does with Magris, who returns home in the evening, lonely amongst the psyllyum, close to the walls of the street dimly lit by the hill of San Vito…[234]

This *reisefieber,* the fever of the voyage, will cause the journalist, the passionate "slow traveller," to repeatedly burn kilometres, either from a bicycle seat or from the windows of a train, to look for his own identity:

> North, South, North West, Grand Central, are but empty words. No one knows anymore what these designations mean; they are surrogate identities. It is the obsession which kills the contents; the *where* that crushes/flattens the *what*...[235]

As soon as he left Trieste behind, escaping by bicycle with his son Michele, Rumiz perceives that something has happened:

> Trieste is soon far away and Vienna already seems near. We have severed the bridges behind us. In front of us, instead, a bridge materializes that previously was not there: it brings us towards "somewhere else" like Arianna's thread, and it is already at our hands.[236]

For Rumiz the East is charged with positive connotations, as a bringer of wisdom and as a reclaimer of a lost identity. Even for the journalist, as with the professor, the east abuts the old Austrian Empire and its river is the Danube, but, while Magris finds in Trieste and in the northeast traces of this past, for Rumiz capitalism has killed everything:

> It has been since the fall of the Berlin wall that the northeast has stopped producing myths and ceased being an Other place–an elsewhere. It no longer serves as the nation's door to the East. Rather, there is perhaps no place that fears the East more than the Northeastern regions. In the northeast they fear the Albanian, not the Nigerian, the Iraqi and not the Senegalese…[237]

Even so, to read his pages, one has the impression that, far from the sweet and melancholy separation of Magris, Rumiz feels himself angrily invested in a civilizing mission with regard to Italy. He seems to indicate a solution to the wearisome search for our roots in the East or to the South. Perhaps just this is the point of connection between Orientalism and the question of national identity, and the road that Rumiz more or less knowingly follows is the only one capable of giving a strong response to a "weak thought." It is in the past and in the preservers of the past that we can find traces of the contemporary identity. Both these authors show us the way to follow. Magris in the contemplation of old Austria finds the roots of the contemporary disease, and Rumiz, more restless, burns up kilometres and words aside a bicycle while re-elaborating and reconstructing the past in the light of the present. We have finally joined Trieste, from which we have departed:

> Trieste, perfect *terminus.* It sums up the worlds that will come. Trieste, Italian in its own way, with the Slavs that arrive on the sea, Orthodox churches, Viennese cafés, an eastern Jewish bourgeoisie, and Turks' heads sculpted over doorways. Trieste, corsair city, where one goes to drink happily even after a funeral, and where, to receive a true benediction, one enters secretly into the church of the Greeks. Trieste, transient city, open ethnic theatre. Like the evening before the departure, in the garden in front of the station. Four gypsies that play for the pure joy of playing. Slovaks, Serbs, and Macedonians with their women that dance already make the Kursturica *Underground.* They tell you that here the adventure begins at the front door.[238]

PART III

STATE OF EXCEPTION:

FICTION FILM AND DOCUMENTARY

CHAPTER EIGHT

PAOLA BONIFAZIO

NORMALIZING SPACES OF EXCEPTION: THE OUTSKIRTS AND FILM IN THE ITALY OF THE ECONOMIC MIRACLE

According to Giorgio Agamben, "the concentration camp is the space that opens up when the state of exception starts to become the rule."[239] In it, the temporal suspension of the normal state of law (i.e. the state of exception) acquires a permanent spatial arrangement. Agamben also maintains that if the essence of the camp consists in the materialization of the state of exception, any delimited space in which the normal rule of law is suspended and the police act temporarily as sovereign, has to be considered as a "camp." For example, he argues that even certain outskirts of the big post-industrial cities have begun to look like camps today (in 1994). In Agamben's words, both the "camp" and the outskirts are "bio-political" spaces in which "power confronts nothing other than pure biological life [naked life] without any mediation."[240] By opening with Agamben's rather controversial idea about the "camp," I do not want to argue for a comparison between the prisoners' experience in the *lager* and the life in the outskirts in the Italy of the economic miracle. Rather, Agamben's theory appears to me as an intriguing heuristic device to use to understand the dynamics of power relationships in the Roman *borgate* or the Milanese lower-class neighborhoods. While a discussion of these dynamics could be conducted in many possible ways, I have selected for this purpose two films, *Rocco and his Brother* (1960) by Luchino Visconti and *Accattone* (1961) by PierPaolo Pasolini. As I will discuss in this essay, these films generate a way of thinking about the outskirts in tune with Agamben's theory of the *spaces* of exception, laying bare the "bio-political" nature of the peripheral spaces of major Italian cities.

While Agamben is concerned with today's re-appearance of the "camp," I am moving backward in time to the Italy of the economic miracle, when government propaganda declared that the country had definitely moved away from the state of emergency caused by War World II. Agamben's definition of the "state of exception," rooted in Carl Schmidt's and Walter Benjamin's writings, is not equivalent to a state of emergency such as a crisis caused by war. However, considering the process of reconstruction in Italy after World War II, the rapport between the "exception" and the "emergency" seems worthy of attention. Before we move to Visconti's and Pasolini's films, I would like to briefly clarify how I make use of concepts like "normalization" (Foucault) and "naked life" (Agamben) in the post-war Italian context. In order to do so, I am again selecting a cinematic text, this time one of several documentary films sponsored by the Italian government[241] during the 1950s in order to popularize the government achievements regarding the country's reconstruction. Among the government's measures to lead the country out of the state of emergency was the construction of new apartment buildings in rural areas or outside the major cities, called *borgate*. In the film *Borgate della Riforma* (1955),[242] a pilot-voiceover flies over Southern Italy and visits some of the poorest areas (Calabria, Lucania, and Puglia), regions in which the state has built several of these *borgate*. *Borgate della Riforma* aims at demonstrating that the country went out of "emergency" and back to "normality" by solving the housing problem.[243] At the same time, the film itself presents this change with similar characteristics to what Foucault describes as a "normalizing" process. "Normalizing" means to compare, differentiate, hierarchize, homogenize, and exclude.[244] All of these steps are present in *Borgate della Riforma.* The inside of the *borgate* is compared to its outside and those who live there demonstrate not only an improved economic condition but also a superior moral status. The pilot-narrator calls the clusters of apartment buildings "modern pretty little towns," in which "the sense of property is sacred." According to the film's commentator, the rural worker who enters the new apartment takes a qualitative step away from a "primitive way of life" and towards "civilization." Normalizing also means homogenizing: all the inhabitants of the *borgate* are equally modern and civilized, just because they live there. Eventually, exclusion from the "borgate" is implicitly equal to exclusion from civilization. On the other hand, civilization is based on *where you live,* your moral integrity based on your living situation. If the *borgate* close the door and leave "emergency" outside their borders, the "space of exception" inside of them opens up: a space in which power confronts nothing more than pure biological life ("naked life," in Agamben's terms). I am not talking about power as an external force but as a form that regulates social life from its interior, such as, for example, in the welfare system. In this sense, *Borgate della Riforma* describes a "society of control" (Foucault), whose normalizing process does not take place through disciplinary institution but is interiorized within the subjects themselves.[245] The film especially re-enacts this form of power in the viewers' relation to the images. The pilot-narrator—that is, the cine-eye—never enters the *borgate,* but speaks for those who live there and establishes what is "normal." The viewers look at the *borgate* from the same point of view of the pilot, enjoying his power of knowledge. At the same time, the viewers also identify with the *borgate* dwellers, since they could be one of them. As Maria Adelaide Frabotta highlights, the governmental films of the 1950s were both "deittic" and "performative:" on one hand they would produce knowledge about the Italian reality; on the other, they would provide the viewers with the tools to live in the reality portrayed in the film.[246] In this sense, I would add, governmental films both provide the audience with the power of knowledge and portray the viewers' power of action, in complete agreement with the government's normalizing plan.

Giorgio Agamben discusses the issue of "normalization" in slightly different terms in his essay "What is a people?" Agamben's perspective is particularly interesting to us because it seems to connect the normalization of a society to the formation of its national identity. The term *popolo* (people), he argues, "Designates in common parlance and in the political lexicon alike the whole of citizenry as a unitary body politic…as well as those who belong to inferior classes."[247] This is what Agamben calls the "bio-political fracture" within the concept of "people," which is the fundamental split in modern sovereignty. "At one pole," he writes, "the total state of the sovereign and integrated citizens and, at the other pole, the banishment—either court of miracles or camp—of the wretched, the oppressed, and the vanquished."[248] In this light, to "normalize" is to fill this fracture by simply eliminating one of its terms, the one that has been arbitrarily marked as abnormal. "Normalizing" Italian society, the *borgate* contribute to the formation of a unitary Italian nation. However, according to Agamben, the fracture between *people* and *People* inherently constitutes the concept of *popolo*—its existence bound to that split. Suggesting that the capitalistic-democratic plan to eliminate the poor reproduces inside itself "the people of the excluded," Agamben reiterates the paradox: "[people] is what cannot be included in the whole of which it is a part as well as what cannot belong to the whole in which it is always already included."[249]

The documentary films sponsored by the Italian government also "eliminated" the poor, in the sense that they literally excluded its presence from the screen. Even in earlier films, compared with *Borgate della Riforma,* such as *045* by Vittorio Sala (1952), indigence is only a transient state. In Sala's film, a family receives from public welfare a comfortable shelter at the new *INA Casa* apartment buildings.[250] Until then, the family lived in a cave at the Caracalla's

Terme in Rome. The documentary films of independent filmmakers, which represented the poor in a confrontational way and challenged the official film production, very rarely reached a large audience because of state censorship.[251] According to director Renzo Renzi, among these films were Fabio Pittorru's *Uomini contro il Po* (1951) and Florestano Vancini's *Delta Padano* (1951), which represent everyday life in the poor rural area around the river Po.[252] Renzi also stated in 1952 about his own film: "The short film *Quando il Po è Dolce,* produced by G.B.Cavallaro and realized by myself, has been excluded from the Venice Festival because it 'denigrates' Italy."[253] According to Renzi, an official bureaucrat claimed that the main problem was that the film was "communist" because it narrated misery.

Excluded from official documentary filmmaking, censored in independent film production, the poor are protagonists of two feature films, PierPaolo Pasolini's *Accattone* (1961) and Luchino Visconti's *Rocco and his Brothers* (1960), both of which came out at the height of the so-called economic miracle. In Visconti's film, the Parondi family is forced to leave their hometown in Lucania and travel north to the industrial city of Milan. The agrarian reform gave them a piece of unproductive land, and no other means to sustain themselves could be found in the area. The film is fiction, and yet it makes a claim on reality, denouncing the failure of government policy in the rural areas of Southern Italy. In addition, the film seems to narrate the process of inclusion/exclusion theorized by Agamben as regards to the concept of "people." At the beginning of *Rocco and his Brothers,* the Parondi family is poor: they are emigrants and they are unemployed. They arrive in Milan and they have no place to sleep. Vincenzo, the eldest son, who emigrated there before them, celebrates his engagement at the home of his fiancé, Ginetta, who is also the daughter of southern emigrants. Ginetta's family refuses to offer shelter to the Parondi, showing no compassion for their *compaesani* (countrymen).[254] Moreover, the two families appear extremely different: Ginetta's is modern, well dressed, rich and enthusiastic; the Parondis are poorly dressed, quiet, and miserable. Rosaria, the mother, declares that her son will not let them sleep in the street, and that he will take care of them from now on. However, Vincenzo himself has no idea about what he should do and turns to Armando, an old Milanese man who guards the construction site where Vincenzo works during the day. The Parondi family will not be let down by "the city of Milan," argues Armando. They only need to find an apartment for which they will not be able to pay the rent. Then, once they are evicted, the city will find another apartment building for them, in which poor people, like them, live. In the film, the Parondis act exactly the way Armando suggested. In order to receive shelter from the city, a shelter that highlights their separation from the rest of the Milanese citizens who either own or rent their apartments, they are evicted: they are rejected, but only to be included in the whole of the Milanese municipality to which they do not belong. In fact, they never did belong to this whole to begin with: the first apartment in which they move (the one which they cannot afford) is in the basement of a lower class apartment building. When they get there, the doorwoman greets the Parondis by urging them to go "down there;" pushing a little cart loaded with their modest belongings, they hurry through the courtyard, while a tenant asks the doorwoman where they come from. "Africa!" she exclaims. Interestingly enough, Renzo Renzi, the Italian director I mentioned above and author of a controversial documentary about poor living condition in rural Italy, also made a comparison between "Africans" and southern Italians Renzi claimed: "we have colonies *in* Italy and it is not necessary Ualual to conquer them."[255] Indeed, it seems that the issue is, precisely, the "conquest" of the poor.

In 1958, PierPaolo Pasolini asserted that the post-war emergency was still an open question: emigration from the South during the 1950s aggravated the living situation in the outskirts of major cities, overpopulating the slums right outside the "borgate."[256] Pasolini also criticized *Rocco* in *Vie Nuove,*[257] arguing that the Parondi brothers were sub-proletarians *di maniera* (manieristic). In this sense, *Accattone* seems to be Pasolini's reply to *Rocco* on the same grounds. The point of contention appears as something other than a solely aesthetic issue about "realism." Pasolini explicitly writes: "Accattone cannot become Ciro."[258] Ciro is the Parondi brother who finds a job at the conveyer belt and is engaged to a Milanese woman. In my opinion, the problem is that Visconti narrates in his film a solution to the bio-political fracture inherent in the concept of people, and Pasolini refuses and challenges the very same solution in *Accattone.* Pasolini's perspective on the poor and the Italian slums of the 1950s is original and *Accattone* offers, in Marcia Landy's terms, "a different vision of the world" (Landy, 176).[259] The key term here from which I would like to begin is *lavoro* (work).[260] The text in which Pasolini criticizes *Rocco* is his response to a letter from a Roman reader, published in *Vie Nuove* in 1960. The reader writes:

> Dear Pasolini,
> I discovered only today that roman citizens are divided in two categories: full-rights and half-rights citizens. I mean the so-called "non-residents," who cannot have residence in the city of Rome because they do not have a steady job, and who cannot have a steady job because they do not have the residence…Overall, for the Roman public administration these people do not exist at all.[261]

Dating back to the Fascist regime, a law that regulated emigration towards industrial cities was still in effect at the time of this letter. According to this law, emigrants could not change residency unless they already had a job in the desired location.[262] However, emigrants could most likely find a job in a place in which they had residency. Eventually, the "existence" of Southern emigrants, according to the public administration of any Italian city in the 1950s, depended on both their residence and on their working situation. The political status of Southern emigrants is linked to work: they lack full political rights because of their nomadic condition, a situation that is viciously perpetuated by unemployment. This situation relates to the analogy between the "camp" and the slum. According to Agamben, the inhabitants of the camp have been stripped of every political status.[263] Interestingly enough, the constitution ratified in 1948 reads that the Italian Republic is founded on work—citizenship is inseparable from work.

According to the government, the poor who live in the slums could acquire recognition and improve their living conditions if they had good will and a positive attitude toward work. This perspective is not totally different from the Marxist one in Visconti's film. In a film such as *Rocco,* work conventionally appears as a means to gain class-consciousness and as an ethical tool to educate the masses. In this sense, I think that Visconti's film is highly influenced by Gramsci's thought, or at least by Togliatti's version of it. Ciro, one of the five Parondi brothers whose story is told in the film, embodies the Gramscian ideal of the "organic intellectual."[264] Thanks to his education, both theoretical (the film stresses the fact that he went to school) and practical (he works in the factory), Ciro is able to gain a critical understanding of the world. It is worth noting that the Parondis finally solve their housing problem by moving to a *casa popolare* (working-class building), most likely because Ciro finds a job at Alfa Romeo. But Visconti's film also portrays work as the "norm" and Ciro as the character who is in charge of its protection. Ciro frequently asks his brothers about their jobs, making sure that "today they worked." The binary opposition between workers and non-workers corresponds to the one between normal and abnormal in *Rocco.*[265] Indeed, Simone is the brother who does not have a "real" job (he is a boxer) and he degenerates, through a chain of events, into a kind of beast, eventually even a murderer. In *Rocco*, work is paradoxically both the sub-proletarians' means to acquire critical consciousness *and* a social tool for normalization.

Pasolini defies both the government's use of work as a "normalizing" tool and the Marxist understanding of work as an element of class formation. His film *Accattone* puts forward the idea that sub-proletarians will lose power rather than gain by means of work. Accattone is a pimp who lives on his partner's income and small thefts. Both he and his friends consider the word work a *bestemmia* (a curse against God). When one day Accattone is willing to change his life and become a "good" person, he finds a job as an unskilled worker. On his very first day, he sighs: "Are we at Buchenwald?" This line opens several questions. In Pasolini's *Accattone,* there is no work as moralizing activity but only labour that, in Foucault's words, "turns the thief into a docile worker."[266] By working, Accattone becomes as a prisoner in a concentration camp. From the government's point of view, none of the inhabitants of the slums are prisoners, since they have the free will to leave the slums and enter the borgate whenever they can find a job. Paradoxically, this is exactly what one can read upon entrance to a Nazi lager: work will set you free! Indeed, the camps were first labor camps. Furthermore, according to Foucault, work is one of the agents of carceral transformation. However, the goal of its use within the prison goes beyond its threshold. Foucault writes:

> What is the use of penal labor? [...] The constitution of a power relation, an empty economic form, a schema of individual submission and of adjustment to a production apparatus.[267]

For someone like Accattone, becoming a proletarian means to acquire a "false" power (freedom from material need), and to submit to the power of disciplinary society. Work disciplines the subalterns and integrates them to its productive system. Accattone's and his friends' contempt for work is a means to awaken us and make us aware of this procedure. Pasolini seems to anticipate Michael Hardt and Antonio Negri's vision of "liberatory politics." As they write in *Empire:* "The refusal of work and authority, or really the refusal of voluntary servitude, is the beginning of liberatory politics."[268]

I would claim that the opposition between Visconti and Pasolini corresponds to the one between the dominant stream of the Marxist tradition and a "neo"-Marxist re-consideration of the sub-proletarian Poor. Hardt and Negri claim in *Empire* that orthodox Marxists always hated the sub-proletarian poor "for being immune to the discipline necessary to create socialism."[269] By stark contrast, Hardt and Negri seem to understand the Poor as "the foundation of every possibility of humanity,"[270] "a liberated life and a liberated productivity."[271] In Pasolini's film, Accattone's resistance to sovereign power is both physical and conceptual. Physically, Accattone refuses to show his ID to a couple of policemen in plain clothes. He tells them: "And why? I did not do anything!" Because he simply refuses to show that card to the two men, Accattone is violently taken to the police station, forced to "speak," obliged to wait for an indefinite length of time without knowing the reason. Conceptually, *Accattone's* characters "live outside of a historical consciousness and specifically, of a bourgeois consciousness."[272] Therefore, they are "pure." Pasolini claimed that the frontality of the shots, the simplicity of pans, and the general "fixity" that characterized his way of "looking at the world of the poor" corresponded to his desire to maintain the "purity" of "the elements at work in the psychology of a derelict." These elements are pure because they are "devoid of consciousness."[273] Accattone's purity is not tainted by nostalgia. This becomes particularly clear in comparison to Stella, the girl with whom Accattone has a relationship while trying to convince her to become a prostitute. When Accattone sees Stella for the first time, he says: "You must be from somewhere else. I would not think you were from Rome. You seem so pure and innocent. *Boh.* You are lucky that you do not know." In this scene, Accattone expresses Pasolini's own nostalgia for an ideal *lumpen-proletariat* embodied by Stella. Accattone, instead, is a sub-proletarian charged with Pasolini's antagonism for "normality" (in the foucauldian sense) and conformism. Accattone's challenge is an absolute human condition as free from work and the state.

I would argue that the sub-proletarians become, in Pasolini's narration, those who *do not want* to become Ciro, i.e. they do not wish to be included in the whole of the Italian people, when this inclusion would simply mean homogenization. Pasolini claims:

> *Accattone* was born in a moment of discouragement, that is to say during the summer of the Tambroni government, so there is a sense in which *Accattone* is a regression with respect to *Una Vita Violenta.*[274]

In this sense, Accattone's resistance clearly appears as more than a local opposition against power. In *Una Vita Violenta,* the protagonist decides at the end to join to the Communist Party. In *Accattone,* the protagonist "develops" from pimp to thief. How could the Tambroni government influence this change? In 1960, Tambroni became Prime Minister thanks to the vote of the neo-fascist party Movimento Sociale Italiano. Several rallies took place against the government, during which the police attacked the protesters, causing several injuries and a few casualties. Pasolini commented in particular on the event that took place in Reggio Emilia on July 7, 1960, and affirmed that the police seemed to kill with an organized and mechanical lucidity, with the same lack of emotion the Nazi police against the Jews.[275] In addition, he thought that the policemen "do not even look like they are Italians;" "the police are an organized, politicized entity, almost the "army of a foreign power installed at the heart of Italy."[276] The inhabitants of the slums, Accattone and his friends, are essentially the same as those people who were killed during the rallies at Reggio Emilia. When deprived of their political status, Agamben writes that "human beings are truly sacred, in the sense that this term used to have in the Roman law of the archaic period: doomed to death."[277] In other words, Agamben argues that in the nation-state, human rights do not exist separately from civil rights. According to Agamben, in the state of exception—when the normal state of law is suspended—the fact that the worst atrocities can be committed does not depend on human rights, but on the individual judgment of the police who act as sovereign. In the case of the 1960s rallies, the police acted as sovereign and could kill the protesters without committing a crime because the state of emergency was declared: the normal state of law is suspended, and the protesters seem not to share citizenship with the police, who kill the protesters without compassion. In *Accattone,* the unemployed and the immigrants, who lost their rights as citizens, rebel against the police who ignore their rights as humans and challenge the constituted power by refusing to work, i.e. by refusing to integrate in society as docile bodies.

I think that we need to look at *Accattone* in the light of the political situation of the early 1960s in order to understand Pasolini's rejection of Visconti's perspective as regards the sub-proletarian condition. *Rocco* links work, political existence and human condition to the sub-proletarian's transformation into the proletarian. Ciro is "human," as opposed to Simone who is like a beast, because he works; work is the binding element for political existence. Pasolini's critique is twofold: on one hand, he argues that the *borgate* (and not the slums) are concentration camps and that work makes docile bodies out of recalcitrant subalterns; on the other, the sub-proletarian does not represent in his film a biological life totally dominated by sovereign power, but a subversive character who rebels against normalization. In 1958, Pasolini explicitly affirms in *Vie Nuove* that the *borgate* are *campi di concentramento* (concentration camps).[278] Pasolini compares the clusters of apartment buildings created by the Italian government after the end of World War II to the Fascist ones, which where built to "redeem" overpopulated cities in the late '20s. They are similar in both architecture and purpose: anonymous, squared buildings aimed at isolating families, breaking up any social contacts among them, providing easy access to surveillance and control for the sovereign power. Pasolini writes: "The borgate of the Christian Democrats are identical to the fascist ones, because they are both founded on the same rapport between the State and the Poor: an authoritarian and paternalistic relationship, profoundly inhuman in its religious mystification."[279] It seems to me that for Pasolini the *borgata* is something like a permanent spatial arrangement for the state of exception. In the outskirts, the *borgata* delimits a "bio-political space" in which power confronts a life made "naked" by the practice of mass consumption and capitalist rule. In his later films, such as *Porcile* (1969), Pasolini will audaciously lay bare the atrocities of capitalism. But already in 1960, writing about the victims of the rallies against the Tambroni government, he declares: "Capitalism reaches today the same level of power and ferocity that it reached before the war: and it is even more dangerous because the catholic-moralists are less idiotic than the fascists."[280] In contrast with the "official" *borgate*, Pasolini sets his first film in the slums. The slums are what he calls *borgate libere* [free], clumps of barracks autonomously built at the edges of abandoned fields, whose roads are nothing more than muddy tracks. I would argue that the vision of the slum aims at triggering the battle against the quiescent and cold ferocity of capitalism, which functions within the apparently securing limits of our own houses. Not only Pasolini's "cinema of poetry" de-stabilizes the viewers' habituated knowledge of the slums by means of its highly stylized realism, but it also affects the viewers, shocking their anaesthetized sense with the flesh and blood of the sub-proletarian world.[281]

Visconti's use of the language of melodrama seems to affect the viewers similarly to *Accattone,* in the sense that both films generate new ways of thinking about the contingent social situation through a form of realism both stylized and "real." I do not mean to deny the differences I previously discussed as regards the issues of work and sub-proletarian condition in *Accattone* and *Rocco and his Brothers.* There is clearly an opposition between the ideological systems enacted by Accattone and by Ciro. I would rather argue that melodrama is a "line of flight" (Deleuze) that breaks through the overt ideological structure of Visconti's film. As Sam Rohdie brilliantly states in reference to *Rocco and His Brothers:* "Melodrama, by theatricalising reality, reveals it while at the same time revealing the impossibility, the unlivability of the emotions it calls up, except within melodrama—that is not in life but in art."[282] In my opinion, Rohdie sees the fiction of melodrama as the place in which the "real" is both suspended and revealed. The exceptionality of the space of melodrama consists in the coexistence of inclusion and exclusion. In this space, the normal rule of law is suspended: according to Rocco, one must understand Simone's violence under the law of honor of the family. By subverting the norm, violence and melodrama in *Rocco,* poverty and laziness in *Accattone,* make the viewers aware of the dynamics of power that govern everyday life. In this sense, I would claim that both *Rocco* and *Accattone* "bring about a real state of emergency," to use Benjamin's expression, in the midst of the normalizing process of Italian society. As I discussed before, the state of emergency that the Italian government claims to have passed at the end of the 1950s is something other than the state of exception as discussed by Agamben based on Benjamin and Schmitt's writings. As I have argued in this essay, Visconti and Pasolini's films seem to represent the outskirts as "permanent spatial arrangement for the state of exception," in Agamben's use of the term. In *Rocco,* work appears as a progressive tool to improve the living conditions in the outskirts, in line with the Communist Party's social strategy; melodrama is what brings about the "real state of emergency." Rocco's devotion to his brother (which Ciro calls "saintliness") subverts the proletarian world of "normality" and work[283]. While Ciro is ready to send away his brother Simone from the family, so that they would be as "normal" as any other family in their working-class neighborhood, Rocco accepts to become a professional boxer (he is willing to sell his body) in order to repay Simone's financial debts and therefore to save the bond that holds his family together. Rocco's action challenges the normalization of the *lumpen-*

proletariat as it challenges the historical development of the Parondi family. Both Rocco and Accattone are not anti-historical but pre-historical: the "real state of emergency" which they bring about is both an awareness that "the state of exception has become a rule" and a different philosophy of history. Rocco's obduracy or Accattone's laziness are productive means to become aware of the bio-power that rules the norm, and to recognize the norm that rules History. As Walter Benjamin wrote, in the eighth Thesis on the Philosophy of History:

> Then we shall clearly realize that it is our task to bring about a real state of emergency, and this will improve our position in the struggle against Fascism. One reason why Fascism has a chance is that in the name of progress its opponents treat it as a historical norm. The current amazement that the things we are experiencing are "still" possible in the twentieth century is not philosophical. This amazement is not the beginning of knowledge unless it is the knowledge that the view of history which gives rise to it is untenable.[284]

CHAPTER NINE

ALAN O'LEARY

ORDINARY PEOPLE (*LEST WE FORGET*)

The spectacle of terror

In a 1989 article for the independent left-wing newspaper *il manifesto,* Giorgio Agamben considers "the spectacle, in other words the politics that we live under."[285] He is referring of course to *The Society of the Spectacle* (1995, originally published in 1967), Guy Debord's influential book where he identifies the mode of late capitalism as that of the spectacular. The spectacle, for Debord, is a development of the commodity form in which everything—politics, social relations, human interaction—is translated into or manifested as image. When understood in Debordian terms, terrorism—otherwise an activity so elusive of definition—is revealed very clearly as a mode of political action proper to late capitalism and, as Agamben points out, one typical of Italy in recent times:

> While terrorism has provided the distracting spectacle attracting a monopoly of attention, Italy has been the laboratory where the transition of western democracy to its final phase of historical development has been tested and implemented.[286]

Terrorist action involves precisely the employment of the spectacle for the ends of political coercion: it is politics as singular impressive event contingent upon the mediatic apparatus of modern society. The September 2001 attacks on New York and Washington, conventionally referred to in the ad-man's sloganistic shorthand of "9-11," were nothing unusual in this respect—rather they represented the seal on an established *modus operandi.* It was not the number or the nature of the September 2001 victims that sanctioned the invasions of Afghanistan and Iraq, and allowed the re-organisation of the global "them and us" around the chimera of the "war on terror;" the licence for the new world order was instead the spectacle of the images of the planes plunging into the Twin Towers. The actions to be taken in the wake of "9-11" were legitimated by the icon of the icons attacked (this is the spectacle as genuine political currency, wired around the world in simultaneous and then infinitely repeated images of the buildings' destruction—the photogenic Twin Towers have, of course, completely displaced the images of a Pentagon less picturesquely damaged). Ultimately the Guantánamo camps, the export of suspects to be tortured abroad, all the paraphernalia of the "state of exception" identified by Agamben were justified by association with these images in belated confirmation of Debord's sarcastic dictum (quoted by Agamben): "Everything that appears is good; whatever is good will appear."[287] The destruction of the Twin Towers seems "good" to us in that sense: the Hollywood iconography (it was a "good" film) releases the gung-ho tactics and Manichean morality of the Bush foreign policy.

The process is not new. As Agamben points out, the political currency of the spectacular was already in circulation in Italy during the so-called "years of lead," when terrorist action dominated the Italian consciousness. The terrorist spectacle was the native mode of what historians call the "strategy of tension:" the clandestine attempt to bring about an authoritarian Italy on the Greek model by fomenting a lawlessness which could then be blamed on communism and the weak democratic state. The casualties and rubble of the unclaimed bombings were intended to function as the very *image* of left-wing irresponsibility, allowing the far-right to assume control in a popular coup.

The most notorious atrocity of the strategy of tension was the Bologna bombing of 1980: at 10.25am on the 2nd of August, a bomb exploded in the second-class waiting room of the train station in Bologna, killing eighty and injuring over two hundred.[288] The city's symbolic importance as a stronghold of the left led early to the suggestion that the bombing was an act of right-wing terrorism. Yet only after many false leads—apparently planted by the Italian Secret Services—pointing to subversive organisations working abroad, it became clear that internal extreme right-wing elements were involved. In 1995, after an interminable trial process, two neo-fascists, Francesca Mambro and Valerio Fioravanti, were found definitively guilty of planting the bomb.[289] They continue to protest their innocence of the bombing while admitting to a host of other subversive and violent acts; the suggestion sometimes made is that they were used as scapegoats for a more institutional massacre, one orchestrated by elements employed by or close to the security apparatus of the state. The Bologna bombing victims' association (the Associazione 2 agosto) remains convinced of the guilt of Mambro and Fioravanti, while also remaining very suspicious of the extent of official involvement in the bombing.

The president of the Bologna victims' association, Paolo Bolognesi, had this to say on the anniversary of the bombing in 2004:

> There are some who wish to erase the memory of the victims of the Bologna massacre. We cannot allow this. Remember that we, the families of those victims, have a duty: a duty to give voice to those dear to us; a voice that denounces injustice and illegality; a voice that demands the complete truth. It is a duty which we assumed twenty-four years ago, and also a duty that the city of

> Bologna took upon itself on the 2nd of August 1980, when we were still digging in the ruins of this station.[290]

The duty of justice is allied to the duty of commemoration in Bolognesi's words. The problem for such a project is that its work risks falling prey to the spectacular prejudice, whereby all that is good appears and all that appears is good—even if what "appears" is the rubble of a train station and the bodies of its dead. The victims' association, in other words, needs to be aware of the possibility that the spectacle of the bombsite and dead may become available as image-currency in the treasury of the partisan right. The terrorist spectacle requires commemoration then, but somehow in ways that elude capitulation to the spectacular. And this commemoration must take place in an image culture where the memory of the bombing will compete with the representation and spectacularization of a myriad other such events. (The project of commemoration seems particularly urgent when we realise that many young Bolognese believe the bomb to have been planted not by the right, but by the Red Brigades, a left-wing formation guilty of many things but never of indiscriminate massacre.)[291] In response to this challenge, the Bolognese authorities and the victims' association have developed what Anna Lisa Tota calls a "poetics of memory display" which necessarily employs the available "memory technologies"[292] in the competitive marketplace for memory. In revealing language, Tota argues that transmission of the memory of the Bologna bombing has been the work of "memory entrepreneurs:"[293] "The [victims'] association has elaborated a kind of marketing project for the sale of the memory of the massacre, as a national asset to preserve and transmit."[294]

The main location of this "marketing project" is the waiting room itself where the bomb exploded. One wall bears a large plaque with the names and ages of the dead. The same site also preserves a small crater in the floor on the spot where the bomb was placed; and the massive gash blown by the bomb between waiting room and station platform has been maintained and glazed. A proposal to place a monument to the victims on a hilltop above the city was rejected in favour of this "commemorative ensemble"[295] in the waiting room. The location in the room guarantees authority and a claim to truth. It is a preserved and embellished wound at the very site of the atrocity itself, so that whatever the judicial machinations, or the false trails laid to deflect from the truth by the Italian secret services, the site itself stands as evidence of the event that will not be denied or disguised. But a fixed ensemble like this can never suffice; even assuming that the space is constantly in use, a memorial is always prone to the contempt of familiarity and the invisibility of indifference. Consequently the "memory authorities" have had to adopt a variety of other means to perpetuate the memory of the massacre and to generate support for their pursuit of truth. Inevitably, one of these means has had to be the moving image, and a particularly interesting example is the short film co-produced with RAI Tre (the most left-wing of the state television channels), *Lest We Forget* (*Per non dimenticare*, Massimo Martelli, 1992). The paradoxical attempt in *Lest We Forget* to commemorate and condemn the terrorist spectacle in an inherently spectacular medium will be interrogated below.

Casualties of civil war

While few would disagree that the Bologna bombing was a terrorist spectacle, the academic writer must be careful with her use of terms. The "terrorist" tag has tendentious connotations in popular and political usage that are unhelpful in academic discourse. "Terrorism" is typically understood as an unacceptable means of pursuing political ends by *non-state* groups. The description "terrorism" always implies a negative judgement of the means, and by extension the ends, of such groups, and so the word inevitably carries a rhetorical ballast of moral outrage which, while it may not be inappropriate, is easily exploited by powers with suspect agendas. Suffice it to point out that the Bologna victims' association would rightly refuse to accept the exclusion of certain state or sub-state groups from the definition of "terrorist," given their well-founded suspicion that the Italian secret services were implicated in the Bologna station bombing and other such atrocities.[296]

A corollary of this is the fact that the discussion of the Italian terrorist years—the *anni di piombo,* or "years of lead"—cannot be limited to the narrow timespans variously allotted to the period. While standard Italian dictionaries typically equate the *anni di piombo* with the 1970s,[297] in Paul Ginsborg's widely read *History of Contemporary Italy* the period dealt with in the section entitled "The Years of the Bullet" begins only in 1976 and ends in 1979/80.[298] Inasmuch as it excludes the Bologna station bombing (to give only the most notorious and pertinent instance), Ginsborg's temporal frame has the effect of concentrating the account of politically-motivated violence exclusively on the activities of a criminalised left. Other scholars prefer to define the "years of lead" as the period stretching from the Piazza Fontana bombing (December 1969) to sometime in the early 1980s, when ruthless police work, repressive judicial procedure and *pentitismo* (when members of proscribed organisations turned state witness in return for reduced sentences) undermined the support base of the subversive organisations on the left. The location of the "origin" of the "years of lead" in the right-wing bombing of the Banca Agricoltura di Milano in Piazza Fontana, an act that left sixteen dead, has the advantage of suggesting that terrorist action was not exclusive to the left, and of drawing attention to the "strategy of tension." However, even this relatively more expansive timeframe can be argued to be too narrow. According to the more ambitious account, terrorism in Italy was a Cold War phenomenon: it had its origins in Yalta and the postwar standoff between the Soviet and American empires. It was, to put it another way, a local-national conflict that formed part of the "global civil war" spoken of by Agamben[299] (following Hannah Arendt and Carl Schmitt), and of course anticipated in the vision of perpetual global war (with the constant shifting of allies and enemies with which we have become familiar) described in Orwell's *1984*.

The international ideological confrontation of the Cold War was famously staged in miniature via the antagonism of the specular powers of PCI (the Communist party [*Partito comunista italiano*]) and DC (the Christian Democrats, [*Democrazia cristiana*]) in the Italian first republic. It was a "cold" international confrontation that became very hot indeed for its local victims. The lives of those dubbed collaborators of the DC "regime" were judged forfeit by the far-left Red Brigades and similar groupings. More devastating, if we may judge these things in terms of mere numbers, were the actions of obscure right-wing ideologues who dictated the maiming and murdering of random victims in bombings in Milan in 1969, in Brescia in 1974, in Bologna in 1980 (to give a non-exhaustive list). The guiding dictum was that cited by Agamben in *State of Exception:* "No sacrifice is too great for our democracy, least of all the temporary sacrifice of democracy itself."[300] The victims of these bombings were ordinary people sacrificed to the idol of anti-communism and to a scorn for the popular mandate masquerading as the defence of the Italian nation.

Ordinary people

In the book *Means Without End* Agamben devotes a chapter to the dual meaning of *popolo* (people), a word which can denote "the sum of citizens as a unified political body" (*Popolo*) but also and conversely, a marginalized part of the populace, "those who belong to inferior classes"[301], or any rate those who are excluded from the body of the nation (*popolo*).[302] If the higher-case *Popolo* is the constituency from which the modern democratic state putatively derives its legitimacy and which it exists to serve, then the lower-case *popolo* is the grouping most likely to be acted upon by that state—whether as an embarrassing deviation to be eliminated, "improved" or punished, or made to bear messages intended for the citizenry (*Popolo*) in its political aspect. The victims of the Bologna bomb, whatever their class or status, age or nationality, were rendered part of the *popolo* in this respect: ordinary people who became the ordinary injured and ordinary dead in a spectacular event staged to sway a fearful *Popolo* towards dictatorship.[303]

In an event like the Bologna station bombing, ordinary people are made subject to the terrorist spectacle; they are made to become the medium of the message. Yet, the very difficulty of ascribing responsibility for a bombing left unclaimed, and the difficulty of discerning the motives and goals of the perpetrators, leads to the obscuring of the victims in the interpretative quest for the meaning of the event.[304] Tota writes that:

> A massacre which takes place in a station also impacts on the collective imaginary because of the depersonalization of the victims that it implies: it is precisely the fact that "anyone could have been there" that makes it so appalling in the eyes of the people.[305]

The depersonalization is an essential part of the spectacle—and it leaves the survivors and the outraged in a peculiar bind: to seek the truth of the massacre is potentially to repeat the depersonalization of the victims perpetrated by the bombers. As we have seen, Tota describes the Bologna victims' association as "moral entrepreneurs"[306] with the obligation of marketing the memory of the bombing in the competitive context of the society of the spectacle. Yet, to remind us of the spectacle of the attack (by means of archive images of its aftermath, for example) is perhaps to re-transform the victims into the anonymous bearers of the bombers' brutal message. This is of course one reason why the names and ages of the dead constitute the body of the commemorative plaque in the reconstructed waiting room in Bologna station: the plaque insists on the identity as well as the diversity of the fallen. But the problem of perpetrating the murderers' agenda persists and impresses itself on the duty of insisting on the memory of the massacre, a task that must be acquitted through various media in order to have any chance of success.

The duties and modes of memory

What, then, is the correct way to represent terrorism on film? What is the duty to the victim and what can the work of commemoration expect from an audience?

The film *Lest We Forget* is part of an effort of memory and commemoration that began very soon after the Bologna station bombing. Tota[307] describes this effort as having two phases: the first, a collective expression of mourning that lasted from the day of the bombing until 1994; the second, from 1995, a phase of moral and civic testimony, and the reinvention of the commemorative ensemble in the station waiting room as a "living monument"—a location for cultural events of various sorts. A fiction film of forty-five minutes, *Lest We Forget* places itself at the cusp of these two phases: it is a work of mourning that also anticipates the period of civic testimony.

In *Lest We Forget,* a fictional survivor of the bombing is seen making his annual pilgrimage to Bologna on the anniversary of the massacre. As he travels (always facing backwards in his train carriage, just as he faces backwards in time) the film visualizes as flashback his memories of different characters in the station, the ordinary people who did *not* survive, living the final minutes of their lives. Filtered through the consciousness of the narrator Giancarlo Lombardi points out that his is the only face shown in close-up, "as if to invite viewers into his head, his reflections, his trauma,"[308] the film becomes a kind of mediation between subjectivity and history of the type described by Thomas Elsaesser:

> Films—some mainstream, some produced with and for television—have proved to be a most extraordinary instrument for giving shape, texture and voice to a "history from below" or "everyday history", at once authenticating "lived experience" through the power of immediacy inherent in the moving image, and demonstrating the cinema's capacity to "fake" such authenticity through the stylistic-narrational techniques of editing sounds and images.[309]

The "faking" or fictional aspects of these films, and of *Lest We Forget,* might be said paradoxically to give them the advantage over the archive and its raw footage. It is salutary to contrast *Lest We Forget* with images of the Bologna attack broadcast as part of the series, *La notte della repubblica,* an 18-part history of terrorism in Italy shown on Italian television in the late eighties. The images shown were captured by two local journalists in the wake of the bombing and in *La notte della repubblica,* are broadcast without voiceover or comment for a full twelve minutes.[310] They show volunteers and emergency workers sifting and digging in the rubble, and corpses being found and removed from the scene. The footage is characterised by a shaky hand-held camera, indistinct ambient noise and the functional use of zoom to focus on a particular detail or to frame some activity. The film is run in slow motion at the end of the extract in order to dwell on the face of a weeping man and to cue the correct viewer response. The images are for the most part allowed to run on without a pause (at one point the cameraman follows a gesturing man between two cars and directs the camera where the man is pointing: towards a corpse lying untouched on the ground), but a significant edit appears when an unseen speaker objects to the camera's presence: "Get out of here! Away with that television!"[311] What is allowed to enter by the relief worker's objection, and by the consequent edit in the footage, is of course the ethical question: that is, what is it that can and should be appropriately represented. We can assume that there was in the rescue worker's objection a sense that certain things should not be shown. But the belief that certain scenes should not be represented must be accompanied and, indeed, challenged by the question of how to ensure the transmission and also the receivability of the memory of the events. In other words, the twin issue that any attempt to commemorate the Bologna bombing has to confront is one of appropriateness (the duty to the victim) and one of adequacy (the necessity for effective communication of the memory to an audience).

Lest We Forget begins to address the issue of receivability through the faces of its cast: it was made with the voluntary participation of familiar Italian actors. Most of these play the victims of the explosion represented in the vignettes of the narrator's memories, each with its bitter-sweet tale of love affairs, bantering friendships, or chance encounters. The shots of the pensive narrator in the diegetic present, and of his flashback memories of the people (with their familiar faces) in the station on the fateful morning, are violently punctuated by images of the rushing landscape before and outside the train. The impression created is of the inexorable rush of time towards the moment of the explosion, something suggested also by shots of the clock-face on the station platform (an allusion to the icon of the station clock famously stalled at the instant of the explosion.[312] What we do *not* find in the film is any consideration of the motives for the bombing, or of the identity of the bombers; the filmmakers resist speculation and interpretation and the event is left intact as *inexplicable.* This distinguishes it from *La notte della repubblica* and other histories of the "years of lead". In these texts, the Bologna atrocity is typically subsumed as part of the narrative of the years from the late sixties to the early eighties, and so the station bombing is presented as exceptional in scale rather than quality. *Lest We Forget* is different: it insists on the rightful place of the bombing, firstly, in the *national* memory;[313] and secondly, by refusing to contextualise the bombing, by not asking why it happened or who was responsible, it insists on the event's singularity, its uniqueness as abomination. Equally significantly, the explosion itself is not shown, nor is its aftermath. As Lombardi has written: "To witness the discomposure of the bodies shaken and disparaged [*sic*] by the explosion would [...] be inappropriate and, in its own particular way, obscene."[314] The film is concerned to avoid precisely this "discomposure" of the victims' bodies in order instead to insist upon the *integrity* of the victims: that is, on the importance of their lives, even if those lives might seem absurd, like that of the mentally ill woman shown in one narrative strand, or squandered, like that of the junkie and would-be prostitute shown in another. The film tries to put back what the contemporary news reports and archive footage had no access to: the quotidian non-news stories, ironically full of small dramas, taking place *before* the major news-event of the explosion.

In contrast to the austere functionality of the filming and editing techniques of the footage shown in *La notte della repubblica, Lest We Forget* is a mix of modernist editing strategies—disjunctive montage, non-sequential chronology, symbolic imagery—and short stories or vignettes potentially of a surpassing banality were it not for the fact that the viewer knows the stories told are about to be brutally truncated. Each of the vignettes is an instance of a particular genre: comedy, melodrama, social realism; the long sequence devoted to a middle-aged adulterous couple is pure soap opera, but set in the actual environs of the Bologna station rather than in the cheap indoor sets familiar from Italian daytime television. To adapt Elsaesser: *Lest We Forget* gives form and voice to various "everyday histories", thereby authenticating "lived experience" through the film's capacity to "fake" real experience through its technical, but also narrational and generic, means.

As this description of the film's sophisticated mixture of modes and techniques might suggest, *Lest we forget* represents a complex response to a traumatic episode. The idea of trauma is invoked here advisedly: we do well to remember that its use in reference to psychic wounds, and still more in reference to the intersubjective rather than individual experience of shock and bereavement, is a metaphorical use derived from the description of visible physical wounds. But it is a trope that has attained particular power in the context of the Bologna bombing: the vertical gash blown in the waiting room wall by the bomb and preserved there as part of the commemorative ensemble is a figure of the literal trauma caused to the body of the station (and by extension to Bologna itself) and to the bodies of the victims. In *Lest We Forget* the figure is revived in the compulsive recurrence to the traumatic event characteristic of the neurotic, here literalised in the narrator's annual return to the primal scene of the explosion; and in this assertion of trauma we begin to discern the essentially political aspirations of a film that might, on inattentive viewing, appear to lack a goal beyond that of commemoration but which instead has very particular designs upon us.

The political designs upon the viewer that accompany the attempt at an ethical commemoration in *Lest We Forget* can be distinguished in the film's mode of communicating the trauma of the bombing. In order to better describe these intentions, it is helpful here to invoke Ann E. Kaplan's identification of four modes of communicating trauma in film:

> 1. The melodramatic: the trauma is communicated via the content and themes, but closure or "cure" is granted by a cathartic ending.
>
> 2. The viewer is vicariously traumatized, typically by horror or by the direct representation of violence: "a potentially negative result in the sense that the viewer may recoil in distaste or terror out of fear of being haunted by unheralded painful images (as in trauma itself) rather than being empathetically or ethically moved".
>
> 3. The viewer is positioned as a voyeur before a spectacle. This may be brought about by the routine reportage of disaster in the daily news or, suggests Kaplan, in a television series like *Holocaust;* arguably, despite the best intentions of its makers, this might also be the case with parts of *La notte della repubblica.*

> 4. The spectator is addressed as a "witness" to the trauma itself—for Kaplan, the most politically useful of the four modes.[315]

This final mode is the same employed by *Lest We Forget.* Thus, Lombardi has written of how the film "asks viewers to bear testimony;"[316] it locates the viewer, through identification with the film's narrator, as an observer/survivor but spares this spectator/witness the scene of the dead and mutilated bodies, and disallows the release of tension that would follow the representation of the explosion itself. (So we come to perceive the trauma but are not made subject to it, nor are we allowed to *enjoy* it: there is no collapse or eruption into the spectacular.) We are called upon to give testimony on behalf of devastated individuals who can no longer themselves speak, and to pay witness to the value of these brutally abbreviated lives.

Faking testimony

Lest We Forget is not a documentary, and the witness-in-the-diegesis, our representative, is an actor whose victimhood is an invention. His testimony is therefore equally fictional; in Thomas Elsaesser's terms, it is "faked." Ironically, this frank faking aids and not hinders the film's political project.

The authenticity of testimony is posited on our sense that a victim is a key and privileged link to the truth of the event itself; that "link" is what the testimony of a witness is meant to achieve. As Robert Gordon points out, the term "testimony"—in the sense of speech by a witness of an event—is a borrowed legal and theological (Christian) metaphor:

> The theology of testimony sets up the founding relation for the working of testimony, that between witnessing and truth, and also a corollary that is by no means obvious but which has a powerful resonance in modern usage, the (redemptive) relation between suffering and truth. ... [The witness in court] speaks the truth, indeed swears to do so, offers an account of a fact or event that he or she has seen that is both *objective*—it comes from this observer or bystander or participant who is not implicated but is present and has seen—and *subjective*—it comes from one person, and is valorised as testimony because of his or her individual presence.[317]

These conditions are borne out by the narrator of *Lest We Forget:* the objective and the subjective find their correlates in the concrete visualization of what nonetheless remains a "fiction." The narrator has suffered a personal trauma—and makes his traumatic return to the station—but also, in the staging (or faking) of his memories, he speaks for the dead who cannot themselves speak. The danger is that the victims may seem to have died for him. As Gordon puts it: "It is the redemptive residue that jars here, the possibility that the survival of the few and the death of the many could be for a purpose, perhaps even for salvation."[318] Testimony, then, treads a thin line between memory, justice and the danger of providing a "false catharsis," in Judith Woolf's phrase.[319]

If false catharsis is avoided in *Lest We Forget*, it is because the film implies that it could have been any of us in the station when the bomb exploded. The film's final images are of silent, ordinary people—presumably passers-by in the station when the film was being made. These images are stand-ins for us, the viewers, at once potential victims and co-opted witnesses of the massacre. The film is an act of mourning that invents the individual victims it mourns as well as its surviving witness, but it is a "directed" act of mourning that also makes witnesses of the viewer; it makes the viewer a key and privileged link to the truth of the event itself. Narrator, victims and viewer are all annexed to the ranks of the ordinary people, the lower case *popolo* that the film wishes (in its insistence on the massacre as national tragedy) to elevate to the status of the citizenry, the *Popolo*.

The film has designs upon us. Despite its low-key tone and a sentimentality present especially in the music, *Lest We Forget* is a furious political document, a denunciation. The agenda it serves is the same as that expressed by Paolo Bolognesi in the quotation above, and it attempts, as Bolognesi advocates, to acquit the duty of memory and insist on the pursuit of justice. It is a testimonial task which the film also requires the viewer to assume, and one enabled by the identification with a narrator and victims who are just as fictional as the virtual witnesses we are expected to become. Ultimately, *Lest We Forget* attempts to use the means of the spectacular in condemnation of the terrorist spectacle itself. Debord writes: "The spectacle is not a collection of images; rather, it is a social relationship between people that is mediated by images."[320] *Lest We Forget* is constrained to use this mediation—the construction of virtual roles and relationships by means of the film image—in order to refuse the spectacle of the station ruins and the bodies of the victims, and in order to frustrate any putatively "good" reappearance of the terrorist spectacle.

NOTES

[1] "The aim of the essay [Benjamin's "Critique of Violence"] is to ensure the possibility of a violence (the German term Gewalt also means simply "power") that lies absolutely "outside" *(Außerhalb)* and beyond *(jenseits)* the law...Benjamin calls thin other figure of violence "pure" (*reine Gewalt*) or "divine," and, in the human sphere, "revolutionary." Giorgio Agamben, *State of Exception,* 69.
[2] Giorgio Agamben, *State of Exception,* 87.
[3] Ibid., 88.
[4] Perhaps the most widely discussed piece of writing in this regard is Judith Butler, "Guantánamo Limbo," *The Nation*, April 1 2002. In response to a statement made by Speaker of the House Dennis Hastert about the "unique" situation of the prisoners, she writes: "'Unique' thus becomes the word that suggests that the law has limited applicability here, that we are not in a situation in which rules regarding humane treatment can be extended universally, since there are exceptions to the universal, and we are dealing with the exception here." Butler implies, I believe, the extension of the law (however flawed or arcane it may be) to those who have been excepted from it, would indeed be a useful and necessary corrective to the present state. In other words, there is some notion that the "exception" sustained by the U.S. government, could be overcome through the application of existing international law. Clearly, Agamben's argument concerning the suspension of law is more pessimistic.
[5] Similarly, Bauman writes of the state of exception as a failure to extend rights to the "*clandestini*" who arrive on the shores of Italy. There has been some outrage, in Italy, about the lack of transparency of the Cpt, as well as local and regional attempts to abrogate them altogether. See Benedetto Varchi, "I contabili dei rifiuti umani," *Il manifesto,* 24 March 2005, 15.
[6] See Weber for an extensive account of ambivalence in relation to the current war on terror.
[7] Agamben, *State of Exception,* 23.
[8] Ibid., 50.
[9] Emile Durkheim, *Selected Writings,* ed. Anthony Giddens (London: Cambridge University Press, 1972), 173.
[10] This passage is followed by a footnote that reads: "I know of no English term thoroughly expressive of *noia* in Italian, or *ennui* in French." Beccaria, *A Discourse on Public Oeconomy and Commerce* (London: J. Dodsley, 1769), 19. It should be noted that these words, like annoy, in English, derive from a completely different root than anomie: *in + odium,* that which is hateful. This distinction seems very important to make in order to emphasize that the "boredom" of anomie is not one of enmity so much as a suspension of law.
[11] Cesare Beccaria, *A Discourse on Public Oeconomy and Commerce,* 20.
[12] Cesare Beccaria, *Elementi di economia pubblica* (Milan, 1822 [1804]), 175.
[13] Beccaria, *Elementi,* 175. This essay is not the place to elaborate on the intricacies of Beccaria's arguments concerning precious metals. We should note that for him,

preferable to gold and silver is iron, "the metal of defense and conquest" which serves to perfect all pleasures of life." Beccaria, *Elementi,* 175. Or rather, Europeans bring iron to Africa, which abounds in various precious metals and other resources. Iron will, because of its usefulness, become a highly sought after item, a universal equivalent, not because it is rare, but precisely because it is useful and common ("di ricerca universale e commune"). Yet we cannot help but notice that the Europeans will ultimately take away gold, which still maintains very special value, in Europe.

[14] Beccaria, *Treatise,* 38.

[15] "Era...naturalmente taciturno e portato alla meditazione... Questo carattere, che in apparenza rassomigliava alla stupidità, fu costante in tutta la di lui vita." Beccaria, Introduction to *Elementi di economia pubblica* (Milan, 1822 [1804]), 2.

[16] "La considerazione usata ai talenti degli individui nazionali, eccita gli uni dal letargo e dal torpore, e scoglie gli altri dal discoraggiamento." Beccaria, *Elementi,* 6.

[17] The implications of this for the twenty-first century market are profound. In his essay "E-money versus sovranità," Zanini writes: "If, in some not-so-distant future, a large portion of the global wealth...can be exchanged electronically...it is possibile that the necessity of a monetary referent beyond commodities will cease to exist, as will the relative system of taxation to which sovereignty is connected." [Se, in una prospettiva non remota, una larga parte della richezza globale...potrà essere scambiata elettronicamente...è possibile che la necessità di un referente monetario esterno nei confronti delle merci possa venire meno, e con essa, possa venire meno il relato sistem di tassazione, a cui la sovranità è correlata.] Andrea Fumagalli, Christian Marazzi, and Adelino Zanini, *La moneta nell'Impero* (Verona: Ombre corte, 2002), 104.

[18] Beccaria, *Elementi,* 268-9.

[19] Karl Marx, *Grundrisse,* trans. Martin Nicolaus (London: Penguin Books, 1973), 226.

[20] "*Being-outside, and yet belonging:* this is the topological structure of the state of exception, and only because the sovereign, who decides on the exception, is in truth, logically defined in his being by the exception, can he too be defined by the oximoron *ecstasy-belonging.*" Agamben, *State of Exception,* 35.

[21] Agamben, *State of Exception,* 83.

[22] Ibid., 84.

[23] Ibid., 85.

[24] Yet we must not forget that the pre-digital market is radically different, not just in terms of the speed, but quality of transaction. As Zanini notes, "The link between new technologies of electronic payments and postfordist society is something more than a simple sociological proposition." [Il legame tra nuove tecnologie di pagamento elettronico e società postfordista è qualcosa di più di una semplice suggestione sociologica.] Fumagalli et. al., *La moneta nell'Impero,* 106.

[25] Marazzi, Christian. *Capitale & linguaggio. Dalla New Economy all'economia di guerra* (Rome: DeriveApprodi, 2002), 33.

[26] Agamben, *State of Exception,* 2.

[27] A special emphasis has been given, especially in the North American context, to the Guantánamo camp. In the context of Italy, the institution of the *Centri di Permanenza Temporanea* has caused vehement critiques, too.

[28] Agamben, *State of Exception,* 1.
[29] Agamben, *State of Exception,* 23.
[30] The theoretical importance of identifying the borders of the exception has been taken up by, among others, Nasser Hussain and Judith Butler. Moving from scrutiny of the rhetorical tropes used by the Bush administration to justify the current "war on terror," Hussain has argued that the notion of the exception is a fundamental paradigm in contemporary politics. It is specifically on the grounds of emergency, for example, that a series of exceptional measures, such as the detention of "political enemies" in the Guantánamo camp, are legitimized. Thus, Hussain concludes, if we are able to define the juridical, spatial and temporal limits that belong to the exception, we are provided with a theoretical tool that can help us to obliterate the logic of the emergency by which the "war on terror" is based. Nasser Hussain has expressed these theses in the talk entitled "Guantánamo, Torture and the Law" held on Wednesday February 9, 2005 at the Doheny Memorial Library, University of Southern California, Los Angeles. In her controversial article entitled *Guantánamo Limbo*, Judith Butler also makes reference to the possibility of identifying a boundary line that separates the norm from the exception. To provide a brief summary, Butler proposes an understanding of Guantánamo as a space located outside both the Geneva Convention and international law. The Guantánamo detainees, for Butler, are held in a state of absolute sacerty, and their condition reflects the "de-humanizing" tactics adopted by Western civilization "to define itself over and against a population understood as, by definition, illegitimate." Judith Butler, "Guantánamo Limbo," *The Nation*, 1 April 2002, 24. It is therefore urgent to produce "a document with international standing that radically extends the applicability" of the detainees' protections and "tries to make good on a promise of universal rights to humane treatment." Butler, 23. In this way, Butler concludes, we can bring the exception of Guantánamo back into the norms of international law.From my own perspective, Nasser Hussain and Judith Butler seem to share a common assumption. They believe that it is possible to ascribe spatial, temporal and jurisdictional borders to the exception, and both attempt to enclose emergency within a boundary-line separating it from the norm. For Hussain, defining the limits of the exception is a theoretical move that helps us to react (and, potentially, to put an end) to both the exception of Guantánamo and the rhetoric of emergency. For Butler, the delimitation of the exception is a preliminary condition to the re-inscription of both the physical space of Guantánamo and the juridical *status* of its detainees into the "universal rights to humane treatment." Butler, 23.In my view, both Butler's and Hussain's attempts to identify and trace the borders of the state of exception amount to a theoretically ineffective—if not counterproductive—move. From a juridical point of view, indeed, it is apparent that for Agamben "the state of exception is neither internal nor external to the juridical order" (*State of Exception*, 23) because it creates "a zone in which application is suspended, but the law, as such, remains in force" (*State of Exception,* 31). And when it is projected in its spatial and temporal dimensions, Agamben also tells us, the state of exception appears as a topological zone of indistinction: "the state of exception is thus not so much a spatiotemporal suspension as a complex topological figure in which not only the exception and the rule but also the state of nature and the law, outside and inside, pass through one another." Giorgio Agamben,

Homo Sacer: Sovereign Power and Bare Life, trans. Daniel Heller-Roazen. (Stanford, California: Stanford University Press, 1998), 37. I would like to add that the search for the borders of the exception seems to be a troubling strategy from a political perspective as well. In fact, an understanding of the norm and the exception as two entities, each of which is external to the other, seems to reproduce an obsolete notion of the border which, being conceived according to old-fashioned models of national sovereignty and juridical legitimization, does not take into account the fact that the contemporary "transformation of a provisional and exceptional measure into a technique of government … has already palpably altered the structure and meaning of the traditional distinction between constitutional forms." *State of Exception*, 2. Let us also consider, in addition to Agamben's work, what Italian intellectual Toni Negri says on the topic in his preface to the latest Italian edition of *Insurgencies: Constituent Power and the Modern State.* Without making explicit reference to theories of exception, Negri argues that in today's geo-political scenario, characterized by the imperial dimension of sovereignty and command, a binary understanding of "inside" and "outside" as two topological opposites seems unable to account for the phenomena that it should explain: "today we are beyond the modern and, possibly, the constituent power. … The constituent power is the last expression of an 'outside' that used to be ontologically and politically meaningful. The constituent power represented the entrance into history of new forces and new desires: it was the sign of an anthropological mutation. From the outside. But today, in the imperial dimensions of sovereignty and command, there is no more 'outside'."Negri states: "oggi noi siamo aldilà del moderno e probabilmente anche del potere costituente ... il potere costituente è l'ultima espressione di un 'fuori' che era ontologicamente e politicamente pregnante. Il potere costituente era l'ingresso nella storia di nuove forze e nuovi desideri: il segno di una mutazione antropologica. Dal di fuori. Ma oggi, nelle dimensioni imperiali della sovranità e del comando, il 'fuori' non c'è più." Negri concludes arguing that "si può oggi forse dire che il concetto di potere costituente sta alla modernità (cioè ad un regime culturale nel quale il 'fuori' esisteva ancora) come quello di esodo sta allo spazio globale." Antonio Negri, *Potere costituente. Saggio sulle alternative del moderno*, 1992; seconda edizione, Rome: Manifestolibri, 2002, 9).

[31] Giorgio Agamben, *Homo Sacer: Sovereign Power and Bare Life,* trans. Daniel Heller-Roazen (Stanford: Stanford University Press, 1998), 133.

[32] Agamben, *State of Exception,* 41.

[33] Ibid.

[34] Ibid.

[35] Ibid.

[36] Henri Lefebvre, *The Production of Space,* trans. Donald Nicholson-Smith (Oxford: Blackwell, 1991).

[37] From this point onward, I will use a different format for each use of *terminus.* a) I will use *terminus* (in italics) to designate the Latin term that indicates a physical means of territorial delimitation. b) I will use Terminus (capitalized) to designate the divinity that, according to Roman historiographers, refused to yield to Jupiter at the moment of its arrival on the *capitolium.* c) I will use *Terminus* (capitalized and in italics) to designate the "shapeless" and "immobile" stone that was left inside the temple of *Iuppiter Optimus*

Maximus at the moment of the building's construction. When referring to all three its meanings simultaneously, I use *terminus* in italic, un-capitalized.

[38] For the *termini* as a means to separate sacred from non sacred space see: Liv. XLV 5 and V 50; Iulian. *Antec. Const.* 21, 5; Front. *De controv. agr.* p. 22 ff. and 57 in *Grom. Vet.* L; Agenn. Urb. *De controv. Agr.* in *Grom. Vet.* p.87 ff. L. For the *termini* as a means to separate the *urbs* from the *pomerium* see: Liv. I 44, 4 ff. For the separation between city and countryside, see: Paul. *Fest.* p. 5 L; Tac. *Ann.* XII 23 ff.; Liv. I 44, 4 ff. For the separation between two or more portions of land belonging to different owners see: Cic. *Mil.* 54; *Acad.* 4, 43; Ovid. *F.* II 640; Horat. *C.* II 18, 23 ff.; *Grom. Vet.* p. 263 ff. L; Isid. *Etym.* XV 14, 3; Dion. Hal. *a.R.* II 74; Plut. *Numa 16.* For the separation between different states see: Plin. *n.h.* VI 139; Ammian. Marc. XVIII 2; Iustin. I 1; VII 1; XXI 6. Besides showing the ambivalent function of *terminus* as both a means to delimit and separate two different portions of land, the case of the *termini urbis* seems also to offer useful insights concerning the relationship between sovereignty, anomy, and exception. These *termini*, in fact, separated the *urbs* from the *pomerium,* but they also delimited an "anomic" portion of land, that had to remain uncultivated, inserted between the city and its walls.

[39] Giulia Piccaluga, *Terminus: I segni di confine nella religione romana* (Rome: Edizioni dell'Ateneo, 1974).

[40] Piccaluga states: "i *termini* [costituiscono] particolari mezzi sacrali tramite i quali è possibile esercitare un controllo su vari aspetti della realtà." Piccaluga, *Terminus,* 115. According to Piccaluga, "the boundary mark, far from being meaningful for its immediate function only, continuously tends to inform the entire reality." [Il segno di confine, lungi dall'esaurirsi nell'adempimento della sua funzione immediata, tende costantemente ad improntare di sé l'intera realtà.] Piccaluga, *Terminus,* 90.

[41] According to Piccaluga, the *termini* "indicated specific spatial and temporal points" that were "never passing through the field, where their presence would have been meaningless." [Il vocabolo indica ... soprattutto nel plurale «*termini*», dei punti ben determinati sia nello spazio... che nel tempo... *mai* passanti all'interno del campo dove la loro presenza non avrebbe avuto senso.] Piccaluga, *Terminus,*105.

[42] Agamben, *Homo Sacer,* 19.

[43] Agamben, *State of Exception,* 40.

[44] For the displacement of the *termini* see: Horat. *c.* II 18, 23 ff.; Iuven. *Sat.* XVI 36 ff.; Dion. Hal. *a.R.* II 74 ; Paul. Fest. p. 505 L: "eum, qui terminum exarasset, et ipsum et boves sacros esse."

[45] Ovid. *F.* II 639-662. See also: Dion. Hal. *a.R.* II 74, 2-3.

[46] In Piccaluga's words, *terminus* "is both the boundary mark and the divinity of boundaries." [È insieme segno di confine e divinità a questo preposto.] Piccaluga, *Terminus,* 106. See also: Ovid. *F.* II 667-684.

[47] For Terminus' in-exaugurability see: Cat. *Orig.* I 25; Liv. I 55, 3-4; Ovid. *F.* II 667-678; Lact. *Epit. Inst. Div.* 16, 3; Serv. *ad Aen.* IX, 446. According to a small number of sources (Dion. Hal. *a.R.* III 69, 5 e Florus *Epit.* I 1, 8), besides Terminus also Iuventas refused exauguration. Augustine adds to Terminus and Iuventas also Mars (*Civ.* IV 29). For Terminus' refusal see also: Lawrence Richardson, *A New Topographical Dictionary*

of Ancient Rome (Baltimore and London: The Johns Hopkins University Press, 1992), 379-380.

[48] Piccaluga states that Terminus "garantisce l'incrollabilità del *Capitolium* dal quale Iuppiter regge la realtà tutta." Piccaluga, *Terminus*, 290.

[49] Agamben, *State of Exception*, 31. Elsewhere Agamben states that "the most proper characteristic of the exception is that what is excluded in it is not, on account of being excluded, absolutely without relation to the rule. On the contrary, what is excluded in the exception maintains itself in relation to the rule in the form of the rule's suspension. *The rule applies to the exception in no longer applying, in withdrawing from it.* The state of exception is thus not the chaos that precedes order but rather the situation that results from its suspension. In this sense, the exception is truly, according to its etymological root, *taken outside (ex-capere)*, and not simply excluded." Agamben, *Homo Sacer*, 17-18.

[50] Agamben, *Homo Sacer*, 24.

[51] Sabbatucci states: "si dimostrava al popolo radunato nel Comizio, che non c'era più un re a qualificare o a definire il tempo." Dario Sabbatucci. *Il mito, il rito e la storia* (Rome: Bulzoni, 1978), 468.

[52] Brelich uses the expression "una specie di «no man's land» temporale." Angelo Brelich, *Tre variazioni romane sul tema delle origini* (Rome: Edizioni dell'Ateneo, 1976), 2:115.

[53] Sabbatucci uses the expression "tempo di nessuno." Sabbatucci, *Il mito, il rito e la storia*, 468.

[54] For the anomic period inaugurated by the *Terminalia*, see also: André Magdelain, *Jus Imperium Auctoritas: Études de droit romain* (Rome: École Française de Rome, 1990) esp. the pages 279-303. While discussing the "anomaly" of the *Terminalia* and the *regifugium*, Magdelain remarkably states that "under a juridical perspective, the intercalary time does not count." [Le temps intercalaire, juridiquement, ne compte pas.] Magdelain, *Jus Imperium Auctoritas*, 281.

[55] Virg. *Aen.* 9, 448; Lact. *Epit. Inst. Div.* 16, 3.

[56] Ovid. *F.* II 671-2.

[57] Agamben, *Homo Sacer*, 28.

[58] Agamben, *State of Exception*, 23.

[59] "Lo stato di eccezione non è né esterno né interno all'ordinamento giuridico e il problema della sua definizione concerne ... una soglia, o una zona di indifferenza, in cui dentro e fuori non si escludono, ma s'indeterminano." Giorgio Agamben, *Stato di eccezione* (Turin: Bollati Boringhieri, 2003), 33-34.

[60] Agamben, *Homo Sacer*, 38.

[61] The *termini publici* were ambivalently given features of both immovability (*gravitas*) and propagability (*propagatio* o *prorogatio*). The displacement of the Roman boundary marks performed in expansionist processes could have been ordered only by who, *rex* or *interrex*, detained the *imperium* (Tac. *Ann.* XII 23 sg). Any other act of displacement of the *termini* was punished with sacerty. See also: Gaston Jourde, *Du culte du dieu Terme et de la limitation de la propriété chez les Romains en Droit Roman. De la péréquation de l'impôt foncier en Droit Français* (Paris: Moquet, 1886), 16.

[62] Agamben, *Homo Sacer,* 29.
[63] Ibid., 169-170.
[64] "Lenin in Inghilterra" was first published as the lead article of the first issue of *Classe Operaia,* January 1964. The essay has been reprinted in Mario Tronti, *Operai e capitale* (Turin: Einaudi, 1971), 89-95.
[65] The process of subsumption is described by Marx in the posthumously published sixth chapter of the first book of *Capital* (Marx 1969). In the *Grundrisse*, the analysis of this tendency reveals the horizon of the capitalist crisis: "In the degree in which large-scale industry develops, the creation of real wealth becomes less dependent upon labor time and the quantity of labor employed than upon the power of the agents set in motion during labor time. And their power...in turn bears no relation to the immediate labor time which their production costs, but depends, rather, upon the general level of development of science and the progress of technology, or on the application of science to production...Labor no longer appears so much as included in the production process, but rather man relates himself to that process as its overseer and regulator...The theft of alien labor time, which is the basis of present wealth, appears to be a miserable foundation compared to this newly developed one, the foundation created by large-scale industry itself. As soon as labour in its immediate form has ceased to be the great source of wealth, labor time ceases and must cease to be its measure and therefore exchange value [must cease to be the measure] of use value." Karl Marx, *Collected Works*, Vol. 29 (New York. International Publishers. 1987), 90-91.
[66] Tronti, *Operai e capitale,* 89.
[67] Antonio Negri draws attention to a fundamental difference between this formulation and the corresponding formulation in *Capital:* in the *Grundrisse,* Marx formulates his argument with reference to the relation between necessary work and surplus work, which allows for understanding the role of the class struggle, whereas in *Capital* Marx argues in terms of the organic composition of capital (the proportion between constant and variable capital), such that the role of the class struggle is lost sight of. See Antonio Negri, *Marx Beyond Marx: Lessons on the Grundisse,* trans. Harry Cleaver, Michael Ryan, and Maurizio Viano (South Hadley, Mass.: Bergin & Garvey, 1984).
[68] Antonio Negri, "Proletarians and the State [Proletari e lo Stato]," in *Books for Burning: Between Civil War and Democracy in th 1070s Italy,* trans. Arianna Bove, Ed Emery, Timothy S. Murphy and Francesca Novello (London and New York: Verso, 2005), 126. Negri's italics.
[69] Resorting to a socio-economic or psychological determination of the subject entails bringing back an element of measure that can only weaken the subject's struggles.
[70] Negri, "Domination and Sabotage [Il dominio e il sabotaggio]," in *Books for Burning,* 265.
[71] See Negri, *Marx beyond Marx,* 59-83.
[72] The first of these laws was the *legge Reale* (named after the Minister of Justice under whom it was passed in 1975), which bestowed wide-ranging repressive powers on the police (allowing for suspects to be detained for up to 48 hours and granting the police considerable discretion in the use of fire-arms). The "legge Reale" was harshly criticized by much of Italy's liberal democratic culture.

[73] On the April 7 trials, see Nanni Balestrini and Primo Moroni, *L'orda d'oro1967-1977* 2nd ed. (Milano: Feltrinelli, 2003), 668; Giorgio Bocca, *Il caso 7 aprile* (Milan: Feltrinelli, 1980).

[74] The expression *teorema Calogero* derives from the name of the public prosecutor for Padova who initiated the investigations.

[75] The charges brought against Negri included 17 homicides, among them that of Aldo Moro, president of the Christian Democrat party.

[76] Agamben, *State of Exception,* 36.

[77] Negri, "Workers' Party against Work [Partito operaio contro il lavoro]," in *Books for Burning,* 87.

[78] The *teorema Calogero* can be seen as the attempt to interpret this concept of the party as an apology, or even a program or manifesto, for armed struggle as it was practised by clandestine groups such as the Red Brigades. In fact, the notion of a separate vanguard that would determine and perhaps accelerate the pace of the insurrection is entirely absent in Negri's work. On the contrary, to take the inititative strategically is the task of the struggling working class. The party is left with a purely tactical function: it is responsibile for transforming subjective and fragmented revolutionary behavior into a concerted attack and defending the forms of proletarian counterpower.

[79] Agamben, *Homo sacer,* 25. Agamben's emphasis. According to Agamben, the ontological theory developed by Badiou in *L'être et l'événement* represents "a rigorous thought of the exception."

[80] The expression "analytic of power" [analytique du pouvoir] is used in Foucault 1976. Foucault does not set out to write a critique of power, but an analytic: he sets out to answer the question "What is power?"

[81] Agamben, *Homo sacer,* 85.

[82] Ibid., 16.

[83] Carl Schmitt, *Political Theology*, 5.

[84] "È un fatto che per tutto il periodo del Medioevo 'germanico' o 'barbarico'...e cioè nel 'profondo e buio alto Medioevo,' la pena di morte, per l'omicidio, non esiste...C'è, al suo posto, il guidrigildo." Italo Mereu, *La Morte Come Pena: Saggio Sulla Violenza Legale* (Roma: Donzelli Editore, 1982, 2000), 12.

[85] Mereu, *La morte come pena,*14-15.

[86]."È questo il momento in cui ha inizio e troverà piena attuazione quella profonda rivoluzione giuridica nel campo del diritto penale e processuale che, con la legittimazione del sospetto, con la creazione del sistema inquisitorio...cambierà aspetto a tutta la legislazione penale e processuale d'Europa, con effetti che durano ancora." Ibid., 19

[87] Jacques Derrida, "Force of Law: The 'Mystical Foundation of Authority,'" in *Deconstruction and the Possibility of Justice,* ed. Drucilla Cornell, Michel Rosenfeld, David Gray Carlson (New York and London: Routledge, 1992), 12.

[88] "Per il Medio Evo si può parlare di Stato di diritto nel senso di Stato che prende autorità e forza dal diritto e da esso è dominato e sorretto...Sovranità non è un concetto politico, ma giuridico, nel senso che rappresenta il modo tipicamente medievale di esprimere l'idea che il *princeps* fonda il diritto perché occupa la posizione sovrana." Diego Quaglioni, *La Sovranità* (Roma and Bari: Laterza, 2004), 24-26.

[89] Walter Benjamin, *Critique of Violence,* in *Selected Writings* (Cambridge and London: The Belknap Press of Harvard University Press, 1997), 1:242.
[90] Benjamin, *Critique of Violence,* 239.
[91] Derrida, "Force of Law," 42.
[92] Benjamin, *Critique of Violence,* 250.
[93] Ibid., 252.
[94] Here the original has it: "et un appel á la croyance." It is completely unclear to me why the British translator has deleted this part of the sentence.
[95] Derrida, "Force of Law," 13.
[96] Schmitt, *Political Theology,* 6-7.
[97] Benjamin, *Critique of Violence,* 250.
[98] Schmitt, *Political Theology,* 33.
[99] Agamben, *State of Exception,* 76 (quoting André Magdelain).
[100] Derrida, "Force of Law," 11.
[101] Agamben, *State of Exception,* 14.
[102] Derrida, "Force of Law," 14.
[103] Agamben, *State of Exception,* 86.
[104] Schmitt, *Political Theology,* 12.
[105] Agamben, *Homo Sacer,* 121.
[106] "Da una feroce reazione politica nessuno, *nessuno*, è sicuro. La guillottina non conobbe amici o nemici; non conobbe né sudditi né re." Carlo Cattaneo, *Scritti Politici,* ed. Mario Boneschi (Florence: Le Monnier, 1964-65), 1:400.
[107] Steve Wright, *Storming Heaven: Class Composition and Struggle in Italian Autonomist Marxism* (London: Pluto Press, 2002) offers the most comprehensive English-language account of *operaismo*. See also Harry Cleaver, *Reading Capital Politically* (Edinburgh: AK Press, 2000), 64-77, and Robert Lumley, *States of Emergency: Cultures of Revolt in Italy from 1968 to 1978* (New York and London: Verso, 1990), 167-270.
[108] "Abbiamo visto anche noi prima lo sviluppo capitalistico, poi le lotte operaie. È un errore. Occorre rovesciare il problema, cambiare il segno, ripartire dal principio: e il principio è la lotta di classe operaia. A livello di capitale socialmente sviluppato, lo sviluppo capitalistico è subordinato alle lotte operaie, viene dopo di esse e ad esse deve far corrispondere il meccanismo politico della propria produzione." Mario Tronti, *Operai e capitale* (Turin: Einaudi, 1966), 89.
[109] "Dentro e contro il capitale." Tronti, *Operai e capitale,* 229.
[110] "Il *take-off* della società capitalistica può offrire l'occasione storica per una rivoluzione a contenuto socialista." Ibid., 67.
[111] "Astensione dal lavoro…è rifiuto del comando del capitale come organizzatore della produzione, è dire *no* in un punto determinato alla proposta del lavoro concreto, è blocco *momentaneo* del processo lavorativo come minaccia ricorrente che toglie contenuto al processo di valorizzazione." Ibid., 237.
[112] "Fate che gli italiani non perdano la voglia di lavorare." Nanni Balestrini and Primo Moroni, *L'orda d'oro 1968-1977* (Milan: SugarCo, 1988), 315.

[113] For an overview of the events of the Hot Autumn, see Balestrini and Moroni, *L'orda d'oro 1968-1977,* 278-348.
[114] For a case study of autoreduction in Turin, see Eddi Cherki and Michel Wieviorka. "Autoreduction Movements in Turin," *Semiotext[e]* 3, no. 3 (1980): 72-79. Autoreduction was practised on a large scale until well into the 1970s, when it was associated with squatting and the *espropriazione* [expropriation] of supermarkets. It constitutes a prime example of the phenomenon of *illegalità di massa* [mass illegality] characteristic of Italy during this period.
[115] In Italy, university occupations began in 1967. On the Italian student movement, see Balestrini and Moroni, *L'orda d'oro 1968-1977,* 171-277, Lumley, *States of Emergency,* 47-142, and Wright, *Storming Heaven,* 89-106.
[116] On these extra-parliamentary groups, see Balestrini and Moroni, *L'orda d'oro 1968-1977,* 349-81.
[117] On the Movement of 1977, see Balestrini and Moroni, *L'orda d'oro 1968-1977,* 504-581, Lumley, *States of Emergency,* 295-312, and Bifo (Franco Berardi), "Anatomy of Autonomy," *Semiotext[e]* 3, no. 3 (1980): 148-71, 155-60.
[118] The mid-to-late 1970s saw a dramatic rise in unemployment in Italy. Bifo (Franco Berardi) cites the official figure for the beginning of 1977 as 1,700,000, noting that the actual figure was probably above 2 million. See Bifo, "Anatomy of Autonomy," 154.
[119] In Marxist terms, this can be described as the process of restoring the primacy of use value over exchange value. Toni Negri has defined *autovalorizzazione* in such terms: "Autovalorizzazione proletaria è forza di sottrarsi al valore di scambio e capacità di fondarsi sul valore d'uso [Proletarian self-valorization is the power to escape exchange value and the capacity of founding oneself on use value]." Antonio Negri, *I libri del rogo. Crisi dello stato-piano; Partito operaio contro il lavoro; Operai e stato; Per la critica della costituzione materiale; Il dominio e il sabottaggio* (Rome: Castelvecchi, 1997), 265.
[120] Bifo, "Anatomy of Autonomy," 155.
[121] In the days following the Milan bombing, 84 left-wing activists were arrested. One, the anarchist Giuseppe Pinelli, died under controversial circumstances after being held for four days without charges being brought against him or lawyers being allowed access. Only two neo-fascists were arrested. See Balestrini and Moroni, *L'orda d'oro 1968-1977,* 440-48.
[122] On the Red Brigades and *lotta armata*, see Balestrini and Moroni, *L'orda d'oro 1968-1977,* 382-472.
[123] For background on the April 7th arrests, see Giorgio Bocca, *Il caso 7 aprile.* (Milan: Feltrinelli, 1980), and CARI (Committee Against Repression in Italy), "April 7th: Repression in Italy," *Semiotext[e]* 3, no. 3 (1980): 172-77.
[124] "La morte di Demetrio Stratos, la fine di un periodo, il '68 considerato ormai esaurito; la distruzione dell'individuo attraverso il rito oppressivo e dannoso del lavoro in fabbrica, il rito giudiziario sentito come persecuzione, il rito collettivo del blackout, dove ogni forma di violenza si scatena nella distruzione sotto forma di apparente libertà, sono altrettante metafore dell'idea di morte che circola nel testo insistente e ossessiva. Morte vista come processo ineluttabile e conclusivo di un

ciclo." Gian Paolo Renello, "Guida alla lettura," in *La violenza illustrata seguita da Blackout* by Nanni Balestrini (Rome: DeriveApprodi, 2001), 211-52.
[125] "Organizzazione di segni." Angelo Guglielmi, "Le techniche di Balestrini," in *Vero e falso* (Milan: Feltrinelli, 1968), 138.
[126] "Una calcolata combinazione che viene proposta, esplicitamente, come scelta tra le infinite combinazioni possibili del materiale linguistico, in un universo tutto formato di mere possibilità e combinazioni linguistiche." Edoardo Sanguineti, "Come agisce Balestrino," in *Gruppo 63: Critica e teoria*, ed. Renato Barilli and Angelo Guglielmi (Milan: Feltrinelli,1976), 111-15.
[127] "I vari frammenti possono dispiegarsi su fogli assai vasti, o squadernarsi su un'unica superficie bidimensionale illimitata, e lì incrociarsi tra loro, collegarsi con la logica del "salto del cavallo," della lettura trasversale, o in orizzontale e verticale, come avviene nei cruciverba." Renato Barilli, *La neoavanguardia italiana. Dalla nascita del "Verri" alla fine dei "Quindici"* (Bologna: Il Mulino, 1995), 70.
[128] In the list of sources included in the appendix to *Blackout*, the author of this letter is cited as "P." Its date is cited as August 8, 1979 (several months after Balestrini's escape from Italy). The letter, which describes a holiday outing and features the phrase "e se ci fossi tu anche [and if you could be here too]," appears to have been written by a family member or someone else close to Balestrini. See Nanni Balestrini, *Blackout* (Milan: Feltrinelli, 1980), 64.
[129] "Lettura trasversale." Barilli, *La neoavanguarda italiana,* 70.
[130] "Panorama grandioso sull'immenso ghiacciaio e le cime scintillanti che lo dominano [...] colori nitidissimi sagome sfrangiare di nuvoloni carichi di pioggia sprazzi d'azurro." "Un azzurro fiume di jeans." Balestrini, *Blackout*, 13.
[131] The concert was originally intended as a fundraiser for Stratos' treatment; it turned into a memorial concert when his death was announced. A recording of the concert titled "1979: il concerto" is available from Akarma Records, La Spezia.
[132] For a more extended analysis of the scheme of composition, see Renello, "Guida alla lettura". For an insightful comparison to serial dodecaphony in music, see Renello, 249-51. It might be noted here that an analysis in terms of the Greek concept of rhapsody might prove no less interesting. Unfortunately, space does not allow for such a comparison here. See Walter Ong, *Orality and Literacy: The Technologizing of the Word* (New York: Routledge, 1988), 13, where Ong points out that the Greek word *rhapsōdein* refers literally to the "weaving together" of songs. He also points out that the word "text" derives from a root meaning "to weave." This sheds much light on Balestrini's decision to base his scheme of composition on the pattern of a patchwork cloth.
[133] "E' solo apparentemente semplice e meccanica, giacché...presuppone una quantità di interventi, di decisioni delicate e di grave momento." Guglielmi, "Le techniche di Balestrini," 138.
[134] "Un'eleganza di ghiaccio." Ibid., 140.
[135] "Nella fabbrica non c'è speranza/ nella città disaggregata dall'immigrazione resa inumana/dai quartieri ghetto dove la qualità della vita è drammatica." Balestrini, *Blackout,* 24.
[136] Ibid., 12.

[137] Ibid., 26.
[138] Ibid., 40.
[139] Ibid., 54.
[140] As if to confirm this parallel between class struggle in Italy and the New York riots, Balestrini includes in the second section a number of passages taken from Antonio Negri's *Dall'operaio massa all'operaio sociale* (Milan: Multipla Edizioni, 1979), a work devoted to the changes in the composition of the Italian working class that occurred during the 1970s.
[141] "Abbiamo intenzione di prenderci ciò che vogliamo e vogliamo ciò di cui abbiamo bisogno." Balestrini, *Blackout,* 29.
[142] "I prezzi sono andati troppo in alto adesso non avremo prezzi quando avremo finito non ci sarà più Broadway...Una donna di cinquant'anni con la borsa della spesa entra nel negozio dicendo oggi si fa la spesa gratis...Su, su, i prezzi vanno su / Prendiamoci la robà e non paghiamo più." Ibid., 28-29.
[143] "Una donna mi telefonò e disse stanno passando per Bushwick avenue come dei bufali." Balestrini would go on to use the slogan "Su, su, i prezzi vanno su..." in his 1987 novel on the Movement, *Gli invisibili,* now reprinted in the anthology *La grande rivolta* (Milan: Bompiani, 1999). On the media reports about La Scala, see Balestrini and Moroni, *L'orda d'oro,* 525.
[144] At one point in the chapter, a striking FIAT worker exclaims: "So we say it's time to put an end to this, what with us producing this remendous wealth here and throughout and the world and them not knowing what to do with it besides wasting and destroying it. They waste it building thousands of nuclear bombs or travelling to the moon." [E allora diciamo che è ora di finirla, che con tutta questa enorme ricchezza che noi produciamo qua e nel mondo, poi oltre tutto non sanno che sprecarla e distruggerla. La sprecano per costruire migliaia di bombe atomiche o per andare sulla luna]. Nanni Balestrini, *Vogliamo tutto* (Milan: Feltrinelli, 1971), 188.
[145] "Diriggi le tue lettere a Nizza di Provenza perch'io domani parto verso Francia e chi sa forse assai più lontano." Balestrini, *Blackout,* 43.
[146] "Perseguitate con la verità i vostri persecutori...Noi dott. Pietro Calogero sostituto procuratore della repubblica." Ibid., 42.
[147] "Vittime della frustrazione per quel '68 passato invano profughi di una politica senza pazienza e senza modestia impegnati in una corsa cieca lungo la scorciatoia del mai più senza fucile...E' un morto ridotto a un muto automa che segue docilmente tutti gli ordini." Ibid., 49-50.
[148] Balestrini takes up his critique of the Italian media in his 1989 novel *L'editore* (now reprinted in Balestrini, *La grande rivolta*), where one of the protagonists speaks of the "trial by press a kind of trial that will become common practice throughout the 70s great public trials in which accusations verdicts and sentences are pronounced all at once and in the heat of the moment." [Processo per mezzo stampa questo tipo di processo che diventerà una pratica corrente per tutti gli anni 70 grandi processi publici sommari in cui si emettono subito a caldo a tamburo battente e in una sola volta incriminazioni giudizi e sentenze.] Balestrini, *La grande rivolta,* 316.
[149] "Dentro quaranta cinquantamila persone." Balestrini, *Blackout,* 58.

[150] "Quaranta cinquantamila persone...La percezione di trovarmi in un nodo della situazione italiana che da anni si presenta irrisolto intatto." Ibid., 58-59.
[151] "Insetti di tutti i tipi nidi di picchi nelle finestre uccellini morti fagiani e colombacci che sfrecciano da tutte le parti...Un sonno continuo uno stato di torpore generale accompagnato da sbadigli...Una comune paura di essere soli." Ibid., 63.
[152] "Inibizione," "gran temporale," and "tanta rabbia." Ibid., 59-62.
[153] "Nei frigoriferi spenti il cibo conservato e surgelato comincia a deperire." Ibid., 65.
[154] "Computer giganti." Ibid., 64.
[155] "Ci fu un gutturale grido collettivo quando le luci si spensero...Centinaia di migliaia di persone cercano di tornare a casa o di trovare un rifugio per la notte...solo la fiaccola della statua della Liberta rimane accesa grazie a un'alimentazione autonoma." Ibid., 66.
[156] "Doveva essere un bello spettacolo da fuori tutti quei fuochi tremolanti sul muro nero del carcere in mezzo a quella distesa sconfinata ma gli unici che potevano vedere la fiaccolata erano i pochi automobilisti che sfrecciavano piccoli lontanissimi sul nastro nero dell'autostrada a qualche chilometro dal carcere o forse un aeroplano che passa su in alto ma quelli volano altissimi lassù nel cielo nero silenzioso e non vedono niente." Balestrini, *La grande rivolta,* 261.
[157] "Ridotto a un muto automa che segue docilmente tutti gli ordini." Balestrini, *Blackout,* 52.
[158] "Perché ha segnato l'inizio di un'epoca e continuerà a ritornare." Ibid., 17.
[159] "In Marx's time revolutionary thought seemed to rely on three axes: German philosophy, English economics, and French politics. In our time the axes have shifted so that, if we remain within the same Euro-American framework, revolutionary thinking might be said to draw on French philosophy, U.S. economics, and Italian politics." Michael Hardt, "Laboratory Italy" in *Radical Thought in Italy*, ed. Michael Hardt and Paolo Virno (Minneapolis, MN: University of Minnesota Press, 1996), 1-10. Antonio Negri writes: "In Michael Hardt's words: the 1960s saw Italy putting into practice the politics that French metaphysics was theorizing at the same time, just as during the 19th century politics was practised in France – as Marx reminds us – while the metaphysics corresponding to that politics was produced in Germany." [Per dirla con Michael Hardt, negli anni Settanta in Italia si fece quella politica che nello stesso tempo la metafisica francese teorizzava: così come nell'Ottocento la politica si faceva in Francia—lo ricorda Marx—e la metafisica di quella politica in Germania.] Negri, *I libri del rogo. Crisi dello stato-piano; Partito operaio contro il lavoro; Operai e stato; per la critica della costituzione materiale; Il dominio e il sabottaggio* (Rome: Castelvecchi, 1997), 17.
[160] "Un tappeto che soffoca gli spalti e scende giù a nascondere completamente il prato...un tappeto di spalle di teste e di braccia che sembra agitarsi a ondate sotto le folate del vento...Una mille centomila voci per comunicare." Balestrini, *Blackout,* 15.
[161] "La Fiat teme il loro oddio per la fabbrica...i capi Fiat non hanno mai visto gli operai ridere e gli viene una rabbia della madonna." Ibid., 19-20.
[162] The term 'exit' is used here in the sense given to it by economist Albert Hirschman. In Hirschman's work, 'exit' refers to a strategy of mass defection, rather than of mere protest. See Albert O. Hirschman *Exit, Voice, and Loyalty: Responses to Decline in*

Firms, Organizations, and States (Cambridge, MA: Harvard University Press, 1970), 21-29.
[163] "Il pubblico si è mostrato in forma diversa e è divenuto una cosa diversa." Balestrini, *Blackout,* 18.
[164] "Il rito oppressivo e dannoso del lavoro in fabbrica." Ibid., 15-18. See also Renello, "Guida alla lettura," 242.
[165] "I giovani da una parte il potere dall'altra...l'universo dei valori d'uso che si scontra con la fabbrica e la produzione." Balestrini, *Blackout,* 20.
[166] The influence of Deleuze and Guattari on the Movement has often been noted. It is also clear that many of the theories formulated in *A Thousand Plateaus* are the product of an extended engagement with Italian autonomist Marxism. Explicit references to Negri and other autonomists can be found in the thirteenth chapter of Gilles Deleuze and Félix Guattari, *Mille Plateaux* (Paris: Minuit, 1980).
[167] For a useful summary of the theory of space elaborated by Deleuze and Guattari, see Edward Casey, *The Fate of Place: A Philosophical History* (Berkeley, CA: University of California Press, 1997), 301-308.
[168] Deleuze and Guattari, *Mille Plateaux*, 594.
[169] Marazzi resided in the USA during the events of 1979. He co-edited the 1980 issue of *Semiotext[e]* devoted to Italian autonomist Marxism in which a number of the articles cited above appeared. The reference to *A Thousand Plateaus* is in Christian Marazzi, *E il denaro va. Esodo e rivoluzione dei mercati finanziari* (Turin: Bollati Boringhieri, 1998), 40.
[170] Such consumer spending has always been seen in highly positive terms by the theorists of *operaismo*. They typically interpret it in terms of a generalized rejection, on the part of the *operaio massa*, of exchange value in favor of use value. Much of *Vogliamo tutto* is devoted to this theme; early chapters of this novel by Balestrini chronicle the arrival of a migrant worker in the Italian north, where he begins to spend the money he earns gratuitously, without any consideration for the exigencies of personal economy. As Balestrini has said *à propos* of these passages: "Work and economic development provide the young worker from the south with money that can immediately be converted into commodities, into things: shirts, jeans, records, pizzas, motorcycles. The significance of these things is completely extraneous to him; he perceives only their material dimension: These things are useful to me, I can do something with them and I like them." [Al giovane operaio meridionale il lavoro e lo sviluppo offrono soldi, che sono immediatamente trasformabili in merci, in cose: magliette, blue-jeans, dischi, pizze, motorette. Ma rispetto al significato di queste cose lui ha un rapporto di estraneità assoluto, esse vengono da lui assunto solo nella loro dimensione materiale. Cioè: queste cose mi sono utili, mi servono e mi piacciono.] Nanni Balestrini, *Prendiamoci tutto. Conferenza per un romanzo. Letteratura e lotta di classe* (Milan: Feltrinelli, 1972), 11.
[171] "La rivoluzione del prezzo del cotone, a suo modo, aveva preparato la rivoluzione del 1848, aveva trasformato...la coscienza di quel popolo fino allora costretto dal salario reale a non generare che la propria morte. Da quel momento in poi il consumismo operaio sarà l'espressione del rifiuto del lavoro umiliante, del rumore delle macchine 'al

quale non ci si abitua mai,' perché mai ci si abitua a non poter sognare." Marazzi, *E il denaro va,* 35.
[172] "Che sia la vendita di macchine a cucire ad ispirare le prime forme razionali di credito al consumo non può passare inosservato." Marazzi, *E il denaro va,* 39.
[173] "L'entrata della macchina da cucire nello spazio familiare privato distrugge lo spazio pubblico di quei collettivi femminili che in America si costituivano attorno al cucito." Marazzi, *E il denaro va,* 39-40.
[174] "La vendita rateale frazionata nel tempo è simmetrica ad un modo di produzione frazionato nello spazio." Ibid.
[175] Ibid., 40. See also Louis Althusser, *L'avenir dure longtemps* (Paris: STOCK/IMEC, 1992), 17.
[176] "Momenti di cooperazione informali e ludici." Marazzi, *E il denaro va,* 40.
[177] "Tappeto di spalle di teste e di braccia che sembra agitarsi à ondate sotto le folate del vento. " Balestrini, *La grande rivolta,* 30.
[178] Il *patchwork* è uno spazio amorfo, informale, un luogo in cui si produce comunicando e si comunica producendo, uno spazio temporale in cui la comunicazione fa tutt'uno con l'atto collettivo del cucire, dando al prodotto finale una forma "pazza," anomala, imprevidibile, del tutto diversa da altre forme di tessitura (come il ricamo) per le quali è invece necessaria un'organizzazione disciplinata e individualista del lavoro. Marazzi, *E il denaro va,* 40.
[179] Marazzi's description of a system of production in which the Habermasian distinction between communicative and instrumental action collapses is evocative of his analysis of the increasing importance of communication under post-Fordism's new paradigm of labor (immaterial labor). This analysis is developed elsewhere by Marazzi and has also been theorized by other autonomist Marxists. See for example Christian Marazzi, *Il posto dei calzini. La svolta linguistica dell'economia e i suoi effetti sulla politica* (Turin: Bollati Boringhieri, 1999), Maurizio Lazzarato, *Lavoro immateriale. Forme di vita e produzione di soggettività* (Verona: Ombre corte, 1997), and Paolo Virno, *Grammatica della moltitudine* (Rome: DeriveApprodi, 2002). If the communicative labor paradigm of patchwork belongs not just to the past, but also to the present, this confirms Balestrini's suggestion that the culture of *autonomia* and *autovalorizzazione* associated with 1968 (and linked by Balestrini to the patchwork motif) "ha segnato l'inizio di un'epoca e continuerà a ritornare." [marked the beginning of an era and will continue to return.] (Balestrini, *Blackout,* 17).
[180] "Metafora della morte." Renello, "Guida alla lettura," 241.
[181] "Negli Stati Uniti sarà la guerra civile del 1861-1865 a siglare definitivamente il passaggio verso l'industrializzazione del settore agro-alimentare, necessaria ad eliminare i margini di autoconsumo che le famiglie operaie custodivano gelosamente accanto al lavoro in fabbrica. Le grandi piantagioni di cotone coltivate da schiavi di colore furono trasformate, dopo la guerra civile, in aziende a mezzandria. Dietro il consumo a credito, dietro l'*hire-purchase* della Singer, c'è la storia delle donne e dei neri agli albori della rivoluzione fordista." Marazzi, *E il denaro va,* 41.
[182] "I capi Fiat non hanno mai visto gli operai ridere e gli viene una rabbia della madonna." Balestrini, *Blackout,* 20.

[183] "Metafora della morte." Renello, "Guida alla lettura," 241.
[184] "Un periodo sì duro e teso ma sopratutto di vitalità e di gioia e di intelligenza e di passione." Balestrini, *La grande rivolta,* 316.
[185] Society in reference to "society" under normal circumstances.
[186] It is important to note the original title in Italian, *La Storia, un romanzo: uno scandalo che dura 10,000 anni.* The novel was written by Elsa Morante (1912-1985) and was acclaimed by critics as a masterpiece shortly after it was published.
[187] Gregory L. Lucente, "History and Trial of Poetry: Everyday Life in Morante's *La Storia*", in *Beautiful Fables* (Baltimore: Johns Hopkins University Press, 1986), 252.
[188] In reference to society during a state of exception, I will use "society."
[189] Elsa Morante, *History: A Novel* trans. William Weaver (New York: Aventura, 1984), 91.
[190] Morante, *History,* 82.
[191] In the original Italian: *È uno scherzo uno scherzo tutto uno scherzo!*
[192] Morante, *History,* 229.
[193] Concetta D'Angelia, "'Soltanto l'animale è innocente.' Gli animali nella *Storia* di Elsa Morante", in *Leggere Elsa Morante* (Roma: Carocci, 2003), 113.
[194] Lucente, "History and Trial of poetry", 251.
[195] Morante, *History*, 443.
[196] Ibid.
[197] Ibid., 441.
[198] Friedrick Barth, *Ethnic Groups and Boundaries: The Social Organization of Culture Difference* (London: George Allen and Unwin, 1969). See especially the introduction.
[199] For Said, the Orient is not only a geographical space, defined by religion, culture and race, but also the way in which this space (the East) is perceived by the other space (the West) because "I certainly do not believe the limited propositions that only a black can write about blacks, a Muslim about Muslims, and so forth." Edward Said, *Orientalism* (London: Random House, 1979), 322. Orientalism becomes, for him, the container of the exorcism in all its meanings, from the most pleasant ones, to the most unpleasant others.
[200] Umberto Galimberti, *Psiche e techne* (Milan: Feltrinelli, 2002), 548.
[201] Ibid., 551.
[202] Francesco Remoti, *Contro l'identità* (Bari: Laterza, 1996), 61.
[203] Francesco Remoti, "L'identità etnica e la sua invenzione" (paper presented at the conference of A.R.I.F.S Onlus [Associazione per la Ricerca di Filosofia e Oltre] "Identità e conflitti nel mondo contemporaneo," Brescia, Italy, November 2002), 6. Unless otherwise noted, all translations are my own. To this fear of the otherness, the power and role of the political propaganda is also worth noting. The movies produced under Mussolini's regime by Lux (i.e. *Camicia Nera*, dir. Gioacchino Forzano, Lux, 1933), the Soviet production of Goskino (i.e. *Sovetskie Igrushky*, dir. Dziga Vertov, 1923) and more recently some Hollywood productions under Reagan (i.e. Sylvester Stallone's *Rocky IV*, 1985) show a strong hero or a strong group, who must be perceived as good by the viewer in opposition with a weak and evil opponent.
[204] Remo Bodei, *Il noi diviso* (Rome-Bari: Laterza, 1997), 123.

[205] For 'weak thought,' *(pensiero debole)* I intend the philosophical current of post nichilism that in Italy has its major representatives in Pier Aldo Rovatti and Giovanni Vattimo.
[206] In Trieste, "everything coexists and it is contiguous. Asburgic kingdom, fascism and forty-five, nostalgical monarchism, nationalism and independentism." Claudio Magris, *Itaca e oltre* (Milan: Garzanti 1982), 282. In this sentence Magris summarizes well the dilemma of a land that rests across three borders and the region's historical and ongoing struggle with identity. Perhaps it is even for this reason that in the last ten years Italian intellectuals start to look with interest to this city, strongly desired during the irredentism and abandoned to its own destiny during the cold war.
[207] Angelo Ara and Claudio Magris, *Trieste un'identità di frontiera* (Turin: Einaudi, 1982).
[208] Ara and Magris, *Trieste un'identità di frontiera,* 96-97.
[209] Scipio Slataper, *Scritti politici*, ed. G.Stuparich (Milan: Guida, 1954), 11.
[210] Elio Apih, *Trieste* (Rome-Bari: Laterza, 1988), 273-274.
[211] Ara and Magris, *Trieste un'identità,* 21.
[212] Ibid., 17.
[213] Ibid., 13. This is even truer today, after the cold war. The Slovenian minority that lives in the Italian territory is completely bilingual. Meanwhile almost none of the Italians know the Slovenian language.
[214] Ara and Magris, *Trieste un'identità,* 30.
[215] Ibid., 56.
[216] Ibid., 28.
[217] See also Guagnini in Apih, *Trieste*, 314.
[218] Of course, the relationship between Slovenian and Italian populations living across the borders was not easy going and simple. Italians and Slovenes developed their own nationalistic feelings in opposition to one another, and against Austria. Under the empire, the creation of a cultural and intellectual community had been possible. It became non-existent after the decline of the empire.
[219] Ara and Magris, *Trieste un'identità,* 64.
[220] Ibid., 22. The port of Trieste has been the centre of the economic and cultural development of the city since the Roman Empire. This was especially true under the Austro-Hungarian rule. An efficient railway connected Trieste with all the territories of the empire. Then, the power of the port and city was at its zenith.
[221] Ara and Magris, *Trieste un'identità,* 41.
[222] Zeno and Guido have two attitudes and offer two different responses to modernity. Apparently, Guido is the winner, with self-confidence and bravery. But, ultimately, he commits suicide while Zeno, the "weak," survives.
[223] "Carso" is called the plateau around Trieste. Istria is a region of the contemporary Slovenia, once Italy. The so-called *Questione istriana* is perhaps the most painful event of Trieste's history. Here, I will briefly re-tell what happened. After the War World Two (1 May 1945), the socialist army of Tito occupied the city and its territories for forty days. During this month of terror, acts of personal and political vengeances were undertaken. People were killed or disappeared. Finally (9th June 1945), the Allied

government took control and decided to split the area in two parts. One, the so-called "A zone" (Trieste, Gorizia and Pola) became Italian while Istria passed to Yugoslavia. People were free to decide to stay in Istria or move to Italy, but they had to leave their houses and their things to Tito. This created a deep laceration between the two ethnic groups of Italians and Slovenes.

[224] Ara and Magris, *Trieste un'identità,* 95. "Giulia," so called because of the Alps, it is the territorial part of the region Friuli in which stays Trieste.

[225] Ara and Magris, *Trieste un'identità,* 106.

[226] Here, I must clarify the meaning of "revisiting past myths." According to Magris, in fact, it is not through the eyes of old nostalgic veterans that we must observe the old Austria. In his book *Fra il danubio e il Mare,* Magris presents his poetic of nostalgia: "I think that any authentic nostalgia must pass through the negation that any 'yes' must pass through the *Caudine* forks of 'no' in order to be authentic." We must remember that the old empire was all but free and that Italy was the idealized dream for the writers and intellectuals that lived in the golden age.

[227] Ara and Magris, *Trieste un'identità,* 113.

[228] Claudio Magris, *Microcosms*, trans. Iain Halliday (London:Harvill Press 1999), 5-6.

[229] Claudio Magris, *Danube,* trans. Patrick Creagh (New York: Farraw Straus Giroux, 1986), 215.

[230] Magris, *Danube,* 206.

[231] Magris, *Danube,* 29.

[232] "Diversi vestiti, diversi bioritmi, diversi redditi. Diverso persino il parlare, tedesco classico a oriente, tedesco americanizzato dall'altra parte." Paolo Rumiz and Francesco Altan, *Tre uomini in bicicletta* (Milan: Feltrinelli, 2002), 62.

[233] Magris, *Microcosms,* 203.

[234] "Un viaggio sul Danubio può cominciare benissimo a Trieste. Appunto con Magris che torna a casa la sera, soletto tra i platani, rasente i muri sulle strade male illuminate del colle di San Vito…" Paolo Rumiz, *È Oriente* (Milan: Feltrinelli, 2003), 91.

[235] "Nord, Sud, Nordovest, Grande Centro, ma sono parole vuote. Nessuno sa più cosa vogliono dire, sono surrogati dell'identità. E'l'ossessione che uccide i contenuti; il *dove* che schiaccia il *che cosa.*" Rumiz, *È Oriente,* 27.

[236] "Trieste è subito lontana e Vienna già pare vicinissima. Abbiamo tagliato i ponti dietro di noi. Davanti, invece, si materializza un ponte che non c'era: porta verso l'Altrove come un filo d'Arianna, ed è già in mano nostra." Rumiz, *È Oriente,* 8.

[237] "E' dalla caduta del comunismo che il Nordest ha smesso di produrre miti e proporre un Altrove. Non offre più alla nazione il suo ruolo di porta d'Oriente. Anzi. Forse non c'è posto dove l'Oriente faccia più paura. A Nordest temono l'albanese, non il nigeriano, l'iracheno, non il senegalese…" Rumiz and Altan, *Tre uomini in bicicletta,* 156.

[238] "Trieste, capolinea perfetto. Riassume sempre i mondi che verranno. Trieste italiana a modo suo, con gli slavi che arrivano sul mare, le chiese ortodosse, i caffè viennesi, la borghesia ebraica venuta da oriente, le teste di turco scolpite sopra i portoni. Trieste città corsara, dove vai a bere allegramente anche dopo un funerale, e dove per farti benedire davvero entri di nascosto alla chiesa dei Greghi. Trieste città di transito, teatro etnico all'aperto. Come la sera prima della partenza, nel giardino davanti alla stazione. Quattro

zingari che suonano per la pura gioia di suonare. Rom slovacchi, serbi, macedoni con le loro donne che ballano fanno già Underground, Kusturica. Ti dicono che qui l'avventura comincia sulla porta di casa." Rumiz, *È Oriente,* 21.

239 Giorgio Agamben, "What is a Camp?" in *Means without End. Note on Politics,* trans. Vincenzo Binetti and Cesare Casarino (Minneapolis: University of Minnesota Press, 1996), 39.

240 Agamben, "What is a Camp?" 41.

241 In Italian, *Presidenza del Consiglio dei Ministri* (Presidency of the Council of Ministers).

242 *Borgate della Riforma,* dir. Luigi Scattini, Documento Film, 1955. This documentary, sponsored by the Presidenza del Consiglio dei Ministri, was shown before Alfred Hitchkock's *Rear Window.* See Maria Adelaide Frabotta, *Il Governo Filma l'Italia* (Rome: Bulzoni, 2002), 115. I was able to screen *Borgate della Riforma* at the Archivio Centrale dello Stato, Rome. The film is part of the USIS-Trieste collection of films and newsreels, both American and Italian, from the years 1945 to 1960. For a general introduction to the USIS-Trieste collection see David Ellwood, "The USIS-Trieste collection at the Archivio centrale dello Stato, Rome," *Historical Journal of Film, Radio and Television* 3 (1999).

243 See also, for example: *045,* dir. Vittorio Sala, Istituto Nazionale Luce, 1952; *Braccia Lavoro,* dir. Giovanni Pieri, Istituto Nazionale Luce, 1952. Both of them can be seen on line at the Istituto Luce Archive website: www.archivioluce.com. For a catalogue and a description of the documentary films sponsored by the Presidenza del Consiglio dei Ministri in the 1950s, see Frabotta, *Il Governo Filma l'Italia.*

244 See Michel Foucault, *Discipline and Punishment*, trans. Alan Sheridan (New York: Vintage Books, 1995), 184.

245 See Antonio Negri and Michael Hardt, *Empire* (Cambridge: Harvard University Press, 2001), 21-24.

246 See Frabotta, *Il Governo Filma l'Italia,* 17. Frabotta uses the words *deittico* and *performativo.*

247 Agamben, "What is a people?" in *Means without End. Note on Politics,* 30.

248 Ibid., 31.

249 Ibid., 32.

250 Istituto Nazionale per l'Assicurazione. Amintore Fanfani, minister of work and social security, designed in 1948 a reform project called "Piano INA-Casa," with the title "Provisions to develop working-class employment." The project intended to create both new houses and new jobs for the working-class. INA managed public housing from 1948 to 1962. For a recent and detailed history of the Piano INA-Casa, see: Istituto Luigi Sturzo, *Fanfani e la Casa: Gli Anni Cinquanta e il Modello Italiano di Welfare State: Il Piano Ina-Casa* (Rubbettino: Soveria Mannelli, 2002).

251 It is worth noting that in 1961, German director Michael Roemer and America director Robert Young entered one of the poorest slums just outside Palermo, Cortile Cascino, and shot a documentary about its inhabitants. Compared to governmental films, Roemer's and Young's film challenges the "miracle" of the economic development. The documentary shows the extreme poverty of the slums, letting the people talk about their

stories, without further commenting on them. In one scene, however, the film makes a statement about the relationship between the inside and the outside of the slums. In this scene, a vendor approaches the camera and asks the directors to touch his merchandise. He says that what he sells is as good as what one can find in the department store. Though a slum dweller, the vendor does not ignore what is going on in the outside world of mass consumption. Rather, the space of the slum (as it is in 1961) is *produced* by the world of the outside. See *Cortile Cascino,* dir. Michael Roemer and Robert Young, 1961.

[252] Renzi's article is quoted in Giampaolo Bernagozzi, *Il cinema allo specchio: appunti per una storia del documentario,* (Bologna: Patron, 1982), 142-143. It was first published as "Quando il Po è Dolce," *Cinema* 92 (1952):62-64.

[253] See Bernagozzi, *Il cinema allo specchio,* 142. The original reads: "Il cortometraggio *Quando il Po è Dolce*, prodotto da G.B. Cavallaro e realizzato dal sottoscritto, è stato bocciato dalla commissione di selezione per la Mostra di Venezia, perché 'denigra l'Italia'."

[254] However, they all show a superficial excitement about the oranges that the Parondi have brought with them from Lucania.

[255] "Ualual" is the name of the Ethiopian water plant, whose attack by Ethiopian army was considered as *casus belli* by Mussolini, who claimed that Italy's war against Ethiopia was an act of "defense."

[256] See Pier Paolo Pasolini, *Storie della Città di Dio: Racconti e Cronache Romane. 1950-1960* (Torino: Einaudi, 1995), and in particular, the essays "I Campi di Concentramento" (the concentration camps) and "I Tuguri" (the barracks).

[257] PierPaolo Pasolini, "Dialoghi con Pasolini," in *Saggi sulla politica e sulla società*, eds. Walter Siti and Silvia De Laude (Milano: Mondadori, 1999), 904. This article was published for the first time in *Vie Nuove*, 1 October 1960.

[258] Pasolini, "Dialoghi con Pasolini," 904.

[259] Marcia Landy, *Italian Films* (Cambridge: Cambridge University Press, 2000).

[260] The italian word *lavoro* can be translated both as work, labor, and job.

[261] "Caro Pasolini, solo in questi giorni ho scoperto che i cittadini romani sono ufficialmente divisi in due categorie: cittadini a pieno diritto e cittadini a mezzo servizio. Mi riferisco ai cosiddetti non residenti a coloro cioè che non possono ottenere la residenza nel comune di Roma perché non hanno un lavoro stabile e che non possono avere un lavoro stabile perché non hanno la residenza... Insomma, per l'amministrazione comunale di Roma questa gente non esiste affatto."Pasolini, "Dialoghi con Pasolini," 901.

[262] Fascist law 1092, article 1 (7 June 1939). It reads that nobody can transfer residency to other cities that have more than 25,000 residents, or in other important industrial cities, unless one is obliged *(obbligato)* by professional occupation, public office, or employment. The law was repealed in 1961.

[263] Agamben, "What is a Camp?" 41.

[264] Ciro is an "employee" as opposed to his brother Vincenzo who works at the construction site, most likely without the same safety of employment.

[265] As Foucault writes: "It is easy to understand how the power of the norm functions within a system of formal equality, since within a homogeneity that is the rule, the norm,

introduces, as useful imperative and as a result of measurement, all the shading of individual difference" (Foucault, *Discipline and Punishment*, 184).

[266] Foucault, *Discipline and Punishment,* 243.

[267] Ibid.

[268] Michael Hardt and Antonio Negri, *Empire,* 204.

[269] Ibid., 158.

[270] Ibid., 157.

[271] Ibid., 159.

[272] PierPaolo Pasolini, *Pierpaolo Pasolini: An Epical-Religious View of the World.* Film Quarterly 4 (1965): 32.

[273] Ibid., 32.

[274] Ibid., 35.

[275] "I poliziotti che sparano non sembrano nemmeno degli italiani [...]. La Polizia italiana, insomma, si configura quasi come l'esercito di una potenza straniera, installata nel cuore dell'Italia." PierPaolo Pasolini, "Dialoghi con Pasolini," 896-900. This article was published for the first time on *Vie Nuove*, 20 August 1960. For a representation of the police in a documentary sponsored by the Presidenza del Consiglio, see *Nell'Interesse di Tutti* (In everybody's interest), dir. Marcello Giannini, Istituto Luce, 1953.

[276] Pasolini, "Dialoghi con Pasolini," 899.

[277] Giorgio Agamben, "Beyond Human Rights," in *Means Without End*, 22.

[278] In "I Campi di Concentramento," Pasolini distinguishes the slums, which he calls "free *borgate* of the poor," and the "official *borgate*," built by the township to concentrate the poor, the unwanted. See "I Campi di Concentramento," *Storie della Città di Dio: Racconti e Cronache Romane. 1950-1960,* 125.

[279] "Le *borgate* democristiane sono identiche a quelle fasciste perche e identico il rapporto che si istituisce tra Stato e 'poveri': rapporto autoritario e paternalistico, profodamente inumano nella sua mistificazione religiosa." Pasolini, "I Campi di Concentramento," 126.

[280] "Il capitalismo ha raggiunto in questi giorni lo stesso grado di potenza e di ferocia che aveva raggiunto prima della guerra: ed era più pericoloso, perchè i moralisti-cattolici sono meno idioti dei fascisti." Pasolini, "Dialoghi con Pasolini," 898.

[281] John David Rhodes's unpublished dissertation, "Stupendous, Miserable City: Pasolini, Rome, Cinema," is a brilliant account of Pasolini's films *Accattone* and *Mamma Roma*, as well as of several of his writings, in relation to the history of representations of urban space in general and of Rome in particular. It is worth mentioning that Rhodes points out that an analysis of Pasolini's films and writings on the *borgate* must take into account his concrete relation to them, i.e. the fact that he did live in these areas. See John David Rhodes, "Stupendous, Miserable City: Pasolini, Rome, Cinema" (New York: New York University, 2003).

[282] Sam Rohdie, *Rocco and his Brothers* (Rocco e i Suoi Fratelli) (London: BFI Publishing, 1992), 23.

[283] I believe that further investigation in this sense could also be considered as regards another Visconti's film, *La Terra Trema*, and specifically as regards the relatioship between the images and the commentary.
[284] Walter Benjamin, *Illuminations*, trans. Harry Zohn (New York: Shocken Books, 1969), 91.
[285] Giorgio Agamben, "Violenza e speranza nell'ultimo spettacolo dal maggio francese a piazza Tian An Men," *Il manifesto,* 6 July 1989, p. 1-2.
[286] Ibid., 1.
[287] Guy Debord, *The Society of the Spectacle*, trans. Donald Nicholson-Smith (New York: Zone Books, 1995), 15.
[288] The details of the bombing, aftermath and trials given here are drawn from three sources: the website of the Bologna victims' association, www.stragi.it; an essay by Anna Lisa Tota, "A Persistent Past: The Bologna Massacre, 1980-2000," in J. Dickie et al., eds. *Disastro! Disasters in Italy since 1860* (Basingstoke: Palgrave, 2002), 281-300, and a book by the same author, *La città ferita* (Bologna: Il Mulino, 2003).
[289] In December 2004 an associate of Mambro and Fioravanti, Luigi Ciavardini, was also sentenced to thirty years imprisonment for his part in the bombing. At the time of writing, the sentence awaits confirmation by a higher court.
[290] Paolo Bolognesi speaking in Bologna station on the anniversary of the massacre, 2 August 2004. Full text available at www.stragi.it (accessed 11 October 2005).
[291] Daniele Biacchessi, "Quel giorno a Bologna: Le vittime e i carnefici," *Il sole ventiquattro ore*, 31 July 2005, p. 10.
[292] Tota, "A Persistent Past," 295.
[293] Tota, *La città ferita*, 127.
[294] Tota, "A Persistent Past," 295.
[295] Ibid., 290.
[296] For a concise account of the "strategy of tension" and the part played in it by elements within the state and by international influences, see Martin J. Bull and James L. Newell, *Italian Politics* (Cambridge: Polity, 2005), 101-4. The topic is treated at greater length in Franco Ferraresi, *Threats to Democracy: The Radical Right in Italy after the War* (Princeton: Princeton University Press, 1996).
[297] "Anni di piombo: nel linguaggio giornalistico, il decennio successivo al 1970, caratterizzato soprattutto in Italia e in Germania da azioni terroristiche." Battaglia (ed.) *Grande Diz. della Lingua Italiana* XIII, UTET. "Anni di piombo: gli anni Settanta, caratterizzati in Italia dallo sviluppo del terrorismo e della lotta armata clandestina." Cortelazzo and Cardinale, *Dizionario di Parole Nuove 1964-1984* Torino: Loescher Editore, 1986, 13/4.
[298] Paul Ginsborg, *A History of Contemporary Italy: Society And Politics, 1943-1980* (Harmondsworth: Penguin, 1990), 379-387.
[299] Giorgio Agamben, *State of Exception,* 2.
[300] Ibid., 5.
[301] Giorgio Agamben, *Means Without End,* 29-30.

[302] As Agamben points out, this dual sense persists in English: "Even the English *people*—whose sense is more undifferentiated—does retain the meaning of *ordinary people* as opposed to the rich and the aristocracy." Agamben, *Means without end,* 30.
[303] Some have in fact asserted that the bombing was a deliberate attack on the *popolo*: "This was a massacre that shocked the collective imaginary in part because of its clear class meanings. As many people have since stressed, this was a bomb that materially and symbolically struck at the working classes. The timing and the place of the massacre…revealed the type of victim that the bomb was aimed at: the typical worker from northern factories, going back to the south to visit his or her relatives." Tota, "A Persistent Past," 283.
[304] Meanwhile, the unfocussed threat of the random bomb, its undefined message of fear, results in a potentially infinite deferral of meaning such that other (incorrect) glosses may supersede the meanings to be rightly ascribed to the terrorist spectacle; so it is that young Italians can come to believe the Bologna massacre to be the work of the left.
[305] Tota, *La città ferita*, 60.
[306] Ibid., 156-157.
[307] Tota, "A Persistent Past," 297.
[308] Giancarlo Lombardi, "Terrorism, Truth, and the Secret Service: Questions of Accountability in the Cinema of the *stragi di stato," Annali d'Italianistica* 19 (281-300): 299.
[309] Thomas Elsaesser, "Postmodernism as Mourning Work," *Screen* 42, no.2 (Summer 2001): 201-302, 197.
[310] ElleU Multimedia have issued six episodes of the series, including that devoted to the Bologna bombing, *Strage alla stazione di Bologna*. The Arcoiris TV footage used in this episode is available at greater length (38 minutes) from the web address http://www.stragi.it/index.php?pagina=associazione&par=video (accessed 11 October 2005) under the rubric 'strage di Bologna 02 Agosto 1980'. Extracts are also embedded in Michele Placido's *Romanzo Criminale* (2005), where a character from the fiction is digitally superimposed upon the carnage, *à la Zelig* or *Forrest Gump*.
[311] In the original footage, there is no edit at this point; rather the camera and its wielder are directed away by a policeman.
[312] See Tota, *La città ferita*, 94.
[313] It is significant in this respect that the narrator himself is not from Bologna and has to travel back to the city for the anniversary, just as the attention of the nation is meant to be focussed on the city by the film itself.
[314] Lombardi, "Terrorism, Truth, and the Secret Service," 300.
[315] Ann E. Kaplan, "Melodrama, Cinema and Trauma," *Screen* 42, no.2 (Summer 2001): 201-204, 204.
[316] Lombardi, "Terrorism, Truth, and the Secret Service," 286.
[317] Robert S. Gordon, *Primo Levi's Ordinary Virtues: From Testimony to Ethics* (Oxford: Oxford University Press, 2001), 4.
[318] Ibid., 6.
[319] Ibid., 7n.

[320] Debord, *The Society of the Spectacle,* 12.

BIBLIOGRAPHY

Agamben, Giorgio. *Homo Sacer. Il potere sovrano e la nuda vita.* Turin: Einaudi, 1995.

———. *Mezzi senza fine.* Turin: Bollati Borlinghieri, 1996.

———. *Means without End. Note on Politics.* Translated by Vincenzo Binetti and Cesare Casarino. Minneapolis: University of Minnesota Press, 1996.

———. *Homo Sacer: Sovereign Power and Bare Life.* Trans. Daniel Heller-Roazen. Stanford: Stanford University Press, 1998.

———. *Stato di eccezione.* Turin: Bollati Boringhieri, 2003.

———. *State of Exception.* Trans. Kevin Attell. Chicago: University of Chicago Press, 2005.

Althusser, Louis. *L'avenir dure longtemps.* Paris: STOCK/IMEC, 1992.

Badiou, Alain. *L'être et l'événement.* Paris: Éditions du Seuil, 1988. Translated by G. Scibilia as *L'essere e l'evento*. Genova: Il Melangolo, 1995.

Apih, Elio. *Trieste.* Rome-Bari: Laterza, 1988.

Ara, Angelo, and Claudio Magris. *Trieste un'identità di frontiera.* Turin: Einaudi, 1982.

Balestrini, Nanni, and Primo Moroni. *L'orda d'oro 1968-1977.* 2nd ed. Milan: Feltrinelli, 2003.

Balestrini, Nanni. *Vogliamo tutto.* Milan: Feltrinelli, 1971.

———. *Prendiamoci tutto. Conferenza per un romanzo. Letteratura e lotta di classe.* Milan: Feltrinelli, 1972.

———. *Blackout.* Milan: Feltrinelli, 1980.

———. *L'orda d'oro 1968-1977.* Milan: SugarCo., 1988.

———. *La grande rivolta.* Milan: Bompiani, 1999.

Barilli, Renato. *La neoavanguardia italiana. Dalla nascita del "Verri" alla fine dei "Quindici."* Bologna: Il Mulino, 1995.

Barth, Friedrik. *Ethnic Groups and Boundaries: The Social Organization of Culture Difference*. London: George Allen and Unwin, 1969.

Bodei, Remo. *Il noi diviso*. Rome and Bari: Laterza, 1997.

Bauman, Zygmunt. *Wasted Lives: Modernity and its Outcasts.* Oxford: Polity, 2004.

Beccaria, Cesare. *A Discourse on Public Oeconomy and Commerce.* London: J. Dodsley, 1769.

———. *Elementi di economia pubblica.* Milan, 1822 (1804).

Benjamin, Walter. *Critique of Violence*, in *Selected Writings. Volume 1 1913-1926.* 4 vols, 236-252. Cambridge and London: The Belknap Press of Harvard University Press, 1997.

———. *Illuminations*. Trans. Harry Zohn. New York: Shocken Books, 1969.

Bernagozzi, Giampaolo. *Il cinema allo specchio: appunti per una storia del documentario*. Bologna: Patron, 1982.

Bifo (Berardi, Franco). "Anatomy of Autonomy." *Semiotext[e]* 3, no. 3 (1980): 148-71.

Bocca, Giorgio. *Il caso 7 aprile*. Milan: Feltrinelli, 1980.

Brelich, Angelo. *Tre variazioni romane sul tema delle origini.* Rome: Edizioni dell'Ateneo, 1976.

CARI (Committee Against Repression in Italy). "April 7: Repression in Italy." *Semiotext[e]* 3, no. 3 (1980): 172-77.

Casey, Edward S. *The Fate of Place: A Philosophical History*. Berkeley, CA: University of California Press, 1997.
Cherki, Eddi, and Michel Wieviorka. "Autoreduction Movements in Turin." *Semiotext[e]* III, no. 3 (1980): 72-79.
Cleaver, Harry. *Reading Capital Politically*. Edinburgh: AK Press, 2000.
D'Angelia, Concetta. *Leggere Elsa Morante: Aracoeli, La storia e Il mondo salvato dai ragazzini*. Roma: Carocci, 2003.
Debord, Guy. *The Society of the Spectacle*. Trans. Donald Nicholson-Smith. New York: Zone Books, 1995.
Derrida, Jacques. "Force of Law: The 'Mystical Foundation of Authority'." In *Deconstruction and the Possibility of Justice*, ed. D. Cornell, M. Rosenfeld and D. Gray Carlson. New York, London: Routledge, 1992.
Deleuze, Gilles, and Félix Guattari. *Mille Plateaux*. Paris: Minuit, 1980.
Durkheim, Emile. *Selected Writings*. Ed. Anthony Giddens. London: Cambridge University Press, 1972.
Elsaesser, Thomas. Postmodernism as mourning work. *Screen* 42, no. 2 (summer 2001): 193-201.
Ferraresi, Franco. *Threats to Democracy: The Radical Right in Italy after the War*. Princeton: Princeton University Press, 1996.
Foucault, Michel. *Discipline and Punishment*. Trans. Alan Sheridan. New York: Vintage Books, 1995.
Foucault, Michel. *The History of Sexuality. Volume 1: An Introduction*. Trans. Robert Hurley. New York: Vintage Books, 1990.
———. *La volonté de savoir*. Paris: Gallimard, 1976.
Fumagalli, Andrea, Christian Marazzi and Adelino Zanini. *La moneta nell'Impero*. Verona: Ombre corte, 2002.
Galimberti, Umberto. *Psiche e Techne. L'uomo nell'età della tecnica*. Milan: Feltrinelli, 2002.
Ginsborg, Paul. *A History of Contemporary Italy: Society and Politics, 1943-1980*. Harmondsworth: Penguin, 1990.
Gordon, Robert S. C. *Primo Levi's Ordinary Virtues: From Testimony to Ethics*. Oxford: Oxford University Press, 2001.
Guglielmi, Angelo. "Le techniche di Balestrini." In *Vero e falso*. Milan: Feltrinelli, 1968.
Hardt, Michael. "Laboratory Italy." In *Radical Thought in Italy*, ed. Michael Hardt and Paolo Virno. Minneapolis: University of Minnesota Press, 1996.
Hardt, Michael, and Antonio Negri. *Empire*. Cambridge: Harvard University Press, 2001.
———. *Multitude. War and Democracy in the Age of Empire*. New York: Penguin, 2004.
Herbert, Christopher. *Culture and Anomie: Ethnographic Imagination in the Nineteenth century*. Chicago: Univ. of Chicago Press, 1991.
Kantorowicz, Ernest. *The King's Two Bodies*. Princeton: Princeton Univ. Press, 1997.
Hirschman, Albert O. *Exit, Voice, and Loyalty: Responses to Decline in Firms, Organizations, and States*. Cambridge: Harvard University Press, 1970.
Kaplan, Ann E. „Melodrama, cinema and trauma.“ *Screen* 42, no. 2 (summer 2001): 201-204.
Klein, Naomi. *No Logo*. London: Flamingo, 2000.

Jourde, Gaston. *Du culte du dieu Terme et de la limitation de la propriété chez les Romains en Droit Roman. De la péréquation de l'impôt foncier en Droit Français.* Paris: Moquet, 1886.

Lazzarato, Maurizio. *Lavoro immateriale. Forme di vita e produzione di soggettività.* Verona: Ombre corte, 1997.

Lefebvre, Henri. *The Production of Space.* Translated by Donald Nicholson-Smith. Oxford: Blackwell, 1991.

Lombardi, Giancarlo. "Terrorism, Truth, and the Secret Service: Questions of Accountability in the Cinema of the *stragi di stato.*" *Annali d"Italianistica,* 19 (2001): 285-302.

Lucente, Gregory L. *Beautiful Fables: self-consciousness in Italian narrative from Manzoni to Calvino.* Baltimore: Johns Hopkins University Press, 1986.

Lumley, Robert. *States of Emergency: Cultures of Revolt in Italy from 1968 to 1978.* New York and London: Verso, 1990.

Magdelain, André. *Jus Imperium Auctoritas. Études de droit romain.* Rome: École Française de Rome, 1990.

Magris, Claudio. *Itaca e oltre.* Milan: Garzanti, 1982.

———. *Danubio.* Milan: Garzanti, 1986.

———. *Microcosmi.* Milan: Garzanti, 1997.

Marazzi, Christian. *Capitale & linguaggio. Dalla New Economy all'economia di guerra.* Rome: DeriveApprodi, 2002.

Marazzi, Christian. *E il denaro va. Esodo e rivoluzione dei mercati finanziari.* Turin: Bollati Boringhieri, 1998.

———. *Il posto dei calzini. La svolta linguistica dell'economia e i suoi effetti sulla politica.* Turin: Bollati Boringhieri, 1999.

Marx, Karl. *Grundrisse.* Trans. Martin Nicolaus. London: Penguin Books, 1973.

Mereu, Italo. *La Morte Come Pena. Saggio Sulla Violenza Legale.* Rome: Donzelli Editore, 2000.

Morante, Elsa. *History: A Novel.* Trans. William Weaver. New York: Aventura, 1984.

Negri, Antonio. *I libri del rogo: Crisi dello stato-piano; Partito operaio contro il lavoro; Operai e stato; Per la critica della costituzione materiale; Il dominio e il sabotaggio.* 2nd ed. Rome: DeriveApprodi, 1997.

———. *Marx oltre Marx.* 2nd ed. Rome: Manifestolibri, 1998.

———. *Potere Costituente: Saggio sulle alternative del moderno.* Rome: Manifestolibri, 2002.

———.*Dall'operaio massa all'operaio sociale.* Milan: Multipla Edizioni, 1979.

———. *Books for Burning: Between Civil War and Democracy in 1970s Italy.* A. Bove, E. Emery, T.S. Murphy and Francesca Novello. London: Verso, 2005.

Ong, Walter J. *Orality and Literacy: The Technologizing of the Word.* New York: Routledge, 1988.

Pasolini, Pier Paolo. "Pierpaolo Pasolini: An Epical-Religious View of the World." *Film Quarterly* 4 (1965): 32.

———. *Storie della Città di Dio: Racconti e Cronache Romane. 1950-1960.* Turin: Einaudi, 1995.

———. "Dialoghi con Pasolini." In *Saggi sulla politica e sulla società.* Edited by Walter Siti and Silvia De Laude. Milan: Mondadori, 1999.

Piccaluga, Giulia. *Terminus: i segni di confine nella religione romana*. Rome: Edizioni dell'Ateneo, 1974.
Quaglioni, Diego. *La Sovranità*. Rome-Bari: Laterza, 2004.
Remoti, Francesco. *Contro l'identità*. Bari: Laterza, 1996.
Renello, Gian Paolo. "Guida alla lettura to *La violenza illustrata seguita da Blackout* by Nanni Balestrini." Rome: DeriveApprodi, 2001.
Richardson, Lawrence. *A New Topographical Dictionary of Ancient Rome*. Baltimore and London: The Johns Hopkins University Press, 1992.
Rumiz, Paolo. *E' Oriente*. Milan: Feltrinelli, 2003.
Rumiz, Paolo and Francesco Altan. *Tre uomini in bicicletta*. Milan: Feltrinelli, 2002.
Sabbatucci, Dario. *Il mito, il rito e la storia*. Rome: Bulzoni, 1978.
Said, Edward. *Orientalism*. London: Random House, 1979.
Sanguineti, Edoardo. "Come agisce Balestrini." In *Gruppo 63:Critica e teoria*. Ed. Renato Barilli and Angelo Guglielmi. Milan: Feltrinelli, 1976.
Schmitt, Carl. *Political Theology: Four Chapters on the Concept of Sovereignty*. Trans. George Schwab. Cambridge, Massachusetts, and London, England: The MIT Press, 1985.
Tota, Anna Lisa. "A Persistent Past: The Bologna Massacre, 1980-2000." In *Diasastro! Disasters in Italy since 1860*. Eds. J. Dickie et al. Basingstoke: Palgrave, 2002.
———. *La città ferita*. Bologna: Il Mulino, 2003.
Tronti, Mario. *Operai e capitale*. 2nd ed. Turin: Einaudi, 1971.
Virno, Paolo. *Grammatica della moltitudine*. Rome: DeriveApprodi, 2002.
Weber, Samuel. *Targets of Opportunity: On the Militarization of Thinking*. New York: Fordham Univ. Press, 2005.
Wright, Steve. *Storming Heaven: Class Composition and Struggle in Italian Autonomist Marxism*. London: Pluto Press, 2002.

Accattone. Dir. PierPaolo Pasolini, 1961.
Borgate della riforma. Dir. Luigi Scattini, 1955.
Lest We Forget (*Per non dimenticare*). Dir. Massimo Martelli, produced by Legami! 1992.
La notte della repubblica: Strage alla stazione di Bologna. Dir. Sergio Zavoli et al., produced by RAI, 1989.
Rocco e i suoi fratelli. Dir. Luchino Visconti, 1960.

Contributors

Elena Bellina graduated in Foreign Languages and Literature from the University of Bergamo and received an MA in English from Youngstown State University. She is currently working on a Ph.D. in Italian Studies at New York University, where she is focusing on the autobiographical genre and postmodernism. She has published on Thea Musgrave and Angela Carter ("Il clarinetto postmoderno di Thea Musgrave e il movimento narrativo in *The Passion of New Eve*") and on Elena Ferrante's literary works.

Andrea Benino is working on a Ph.D. in Philosophy at the University of Turin, Italy. He holds a BA in philosophy from the same institution. As an undergraduate he wrote an honours thesis on the Situationist International titled "Il superamento dell'estetica nella teoria rivoluzionaria: l'Internazionale situazionista." He is interested in a variety of subjects including post-structuralism, Deleuze's thought, the relationship between ontology and new form of politics.

Paola Bonifazio graduated in *Lettere Moderne* (2000) at the Catholic University of Milan with a concentration on film studies. She received a M.A. in Italian Studies and an M.A. Certificate in Film Studies at the University of Pittsburgh (2003). She is currently working towards her Ph.D. at New York University. Her dissertation project focuses on documentary films sponsored by the U.S. and the Italian governments during the 1950s.

Marisa Giorgi received her MA in Italian Literature from the University of Pittsburgh in April of 2004. She teaches as an adjunct professor for the Italian Department of New York University. She is currently working on a Ph.D. in Comparative Literature at the Graduate Center of the City University of New York.

Max Henninger received his Ph.D. in Comparative Literature from the City University of New York Graduate Center in 2004. He has taught at Brooklyn College, Queens College, and the City College of New York. His articles "Recurrence, Retrieval, Spectrality: History and the Promise of Justice in Adriano Sofri's *L'ombra di Moro*" and "The Postponed Revolution: Reading Italian Insurrectionary Leftism as Generational Conflict" are forthcoming in *Italian Culture* and *Italica.*

Paolo Matteucci is working on his Ph.D. in Comparative Literature at the University of Southern California. He is currently working on a comparative reading of Ovid's *Metamorphoses* (c. 8 CE), Benvenuto Cellini's unconventional autobiography titled *Vita* (c. 1558), and PierPaolo Pasolini's last, unfinished literary work *Petrolio* (1975)

Alan O'Leary is a lecturer of Italian Cinema and Studies at the University of Leeds. He has a BA degree in fine art and another in English and Italian literature from Trinity College, Dublin. He has an MPhil in European Literature from the University of

Cambridge, and is currently completing a Ph.D. at Cambridge on the representation of political violence in Italian cinema.

KAREN PINKUS is Professor of French, Italian, and Comparative Literature, at the University of Southern California, where she also chairs the Department of French and Italian. Her most recent book is *The Montesi Scandal. The Death of Wilma Montesi and the Birth of the Paparazzi in Fellini's Rome* (Univ. of Chicago Press, 2003). She is currently completing a book that examines alchemy, from the early modern period through the digital age.

CHIARA SARTORI graduated from the University of Trieste in 1999/2000 in Philosophy. At the moment she is working on a Ph.D. in Italian Studies at Brown University. Her dissertation project is an interdisciplinary work on the contemporary ethnicity of Gorizia.

MAURIZIO VITO is a Ph.D. student at University of California, Berkeley. He graduated in Philosophy from the University of Verona (Italy) and received an MA in Italian Studies from the University of Pittsburgh. His main interests are Aesthetics and Political Philosophy. His current research focuses on the concatenations between literature and politics in Italian culture.

INDEX